WHO'S MY ENEMY?

BY

IVAN LYNN BOWMAN

WHO'S MY ENEMY?

Published by Bowman's Books, P.O. Box 452, Hilger, MT 59451
(406) 462-5662
bowman@mtintouch.net

Second Edition

Library of Congress Catalogue Number: 2006908750
ISBN: 0615133827

Acknowledgements: Cover photo montage, and montages on pages X, XVI, XXIII, XXIV, 14, 127 include author photos and images © Jupiter Images. Photo on page 154 © Jupiter Images; map on page 187, photo on page 188, U.S. Army language chart on page 199, courtesy of *Uptight* magazine (Summer 1969). All other photos by the author.

Design, layout, cover and photo montages by Jannetje Anita Thomas
Assisted by Janiece Rustin, Binding Plus;
information@bindingplus.com

A special thanks to Dan Bessie and Jeanne Johnson for assisting in editing.

Printed in the United States of America

WHO'S MY ENEMY?

BY

IVAN LYNN BOWMAN

CONTENTS

WHO'S MY ENEMY?

FOREWORD

DALE A. BURK

One learned in a hurry when arriving "in country" that it didn't pay to become philosophical – in a serious sense anyway – about what you were doing there, particularly if you were an infantryman, a grunt, a small cog in something that, you were told, was much, much bigger than yourself. Or any individual for that matter. Just do your job. Stay alive. Stay alive, serve your time. Stuff all the muck and sweat and grime deeper and deeper into your soul and leave both the questions and answers to those higher up the ladder. Just stay alive. Get back home!

And yet, even during those dark days and darker moments when you had simplified your time to just that, staying alive, you come to the realization that things were never going to be simple or clear or trustworthy again. Your very being is absorbed with thought, deep thought, about who you are and where you are and what you are doing, endless, mind-numbing, agonizing thought wracked by an inescapable sense of powerlessness – of knowing that the war you're waging isn't simply against an enemy on the ground, out there a few unseeing yards in the jungle, but against horrendous unknowns, unexpected and unseen powers that literally control not only your life but your very destiny.

Who, indeed, are these enemies of the foot soldier, and of author Ivan Lynn Bowman in particular? He expands the context of our thought about war, and the Vietnam War in particular, by the single expression he chose for the title of his book: "Who's My Enemy?" What we learn in the pages of this incredibly raw and sharply-honed – so sharp, in fact, in its honest and unvarnished approach to laying out the oft-overlooked story of the little guy on the combat field, the foot soldier or grunt as he was called in Vietnam that we know beyond a shadow of doubt that Lynn Bowman was there, that this, indeed, is a man whose life demanded of him, should he survive, that this story be told.

Well, in spite of all the horrors he encountered as a "soldier" of the United States of America, Lynn Bowman survived. But those seemingly endless months that he spent in Vietnam exacted their toll on him, as it did on thousands of others who fought alongside or with him during those darkest of days and months. *Who's My Enemy?* is a very personal, deeply philosophical and yet – and herein lies its strength – an insight into the vagaries of that time by a very commonsensical, down-to-earth, realistic, young man whose values were shaped, and remained steadfast, because of his bringing up back home in the mountainous regions of his beloved California. This book is an expression of a man whose conscience would not allow him to be corrupted by the horrors of war.

Author Bowman likes to say of his book that, unlike most other Vietman-era titles, *Who's My Enemy?* spares no one, and in particular it challenges the professional military commanders and others who are often fascinated with war-time experiences and life at the expense of the common foot soldier. One comment Bowman has made deserves special emphasis here: "I come down hard on U.S. Army lifers whose bureaucratic thinking made an already murderous slog even harder," he writes. His story also brutally, if accurately, questions the military minds in Washington – and historical hindsight supports him there – and often thoughtless if well-meaning flower children who opposed the war, plus such factors as the use of the defoliant Agent Orange. You will find, however, that he doesn't spare himself, either. From horrific episodes of survival and death to mundane, even stupid as he writes, incidents involving the black market and going AWOL, Lynn Bowman manages to bring the deepest of philosophical concerns about war and those who wage it down to the level, ultimately, where we all reside – right in the middle of coping momentarily with threats to life and limb, indeed the quest for survival, a quest in search of meaning and, hopefully, understanding, let alone truth.

No, Lynn Bowman doesn't spare himself in this book – and that's good because within its pages we find him struggling not only to survive during the war, but later with the effect the Vietnam War had on him, on his country, and, in a very real sense all the rest of us who live in its aftermath. We go with him, within these pages, to the Wall, the Vietnam War Memorial, in Washington, D.C., and along with him we weep and maybe, just maybe, heal a bit, too. If so, we can thank Lynn Bowman for that. *"Who's My Enemy?"* takes us to that Wall with a degree of profound personal involvement and a sense of horror that turns to reverence, even awe because we know that while we pay proper homage to those who died in Vietnam at the Wall, many thousands of others who continue to fight the enemies they encountered in that tragic war aren't listed on that memorial. For them, for Lynn Bowman and his compatriots who served "in country" – like my Air Force fighter pilot brother and my Army grunt cousin, who were there and who still ask the same questions Lynn Bowman does about "who's my enemy?" The story told in this book may be Lynn Bowman's story, but in a very real sense it's also their story told from an often-overlooked perspective. It's just downright illuminating and, I believe, to quote an author I came to respect very much in the reading of this story, Lynn Bowman, "it's a gutsy and informative read" – a personal, inquiry into a tragic episode in the life of an entire nation let alone a deep-thinking Army draftee who has helped us to understand much more about such things.

Dale A. Burk
Nieman Fellow,
Harvard University, 1975-76

WHO'S MY ENEMY?

IN MEMORY

I dedicate this book to the memory of all Vietnam veterans, especially those from my alma mater, Amador High School in the town of Sutter Creek, and those from the entire Mother Lode League of Northern California.

We were young in the early 1960s, full of piss and vinegar, eager to participate in every sport. We put body and soul into anything we tried, did our best and won much more than we lost. But were totally unprepared for what lay ahead. Even our wonderful track and football coach, Coach Davis, an understanding gentle giant with a heart to match, was a second father to many of us. He usually called a player "Son", and we all called him "Coach." He couldn't prepare us for what was coming. But had he known, he sure as hell would have tried.

So I dedicate this book to Coach Davis too. And to Freddie Williams, who sunk down in embarrassment one day in front of the entire team when Davis gently but firmly said, "Son, if you wanna play football. . . in fact, if you don't wanna get expelled, you've got to get better grades." He was talking to Freddie, but in fact he was talking to all of us. Shaken, Freddie not only brought up his grades (as did we all) but also became Amador High's star athlete.

Freddie's gone now, his bright white socks no longer flashing down the track as they used to when he ran the 100, 220 or 440-yard dashes, as well as the exciting relays. Athletically coordinated and fast as Freddie was, he couldn't dodge or outrun the rigors of hell that was

Vietnam. Along with so many other brave souls, his precious young life was snuffed out in the war. What a shame. What a waste. Like Freddie, many of the boys I knew are now only a memory. But the broken hearts and shattered families remain, with our only tangible tribute to them a name on monuments of stone, brass or bronze.

I hated that war that took so many of my friends. Let us pray that we never need, never have, another war like that in Vietnam.

Ivan Lynn Bowman

1

---

[1] If you are ever in town, stop by and pay tribute to these young men that I had the privilege of knowing at Amador High School. The honorable memorial is located on State Highway 49 in historic Sutter Creek, California.

INTRODUCTION

This story comes out of the Vietnam War. The deeds, events, travels and opinions are told from my own point of view and without apology. I don't pretend to speak for other soldiers or for anyone else, and I'm not the "Every Soldier" who fought in Vietnam. I'm just me. The book has been written from my recollection of the war and from my emerging storehouse of memories. From my treks, duties and activities prior to, during and after the war in Vietnam. Many other brave soldiers have their own stories, memories and opinions.

Because of my vigorous travel and duty assignments while in Vietnam, and not having been assigned to the usual GI troop combat duty what you read here may differ slightly from books or stories by soldiers who served their time with larger American units. Right off, I want to state, without prejudice, that nothing I say here should be construed as a criticism or belittlement of the brave American soldiers who were caught up in their own vicious struggles and frustrations while devoting their time and energy and giving all they had.

Who's My Enemy? is mainly drawn from my experiences in and around Bien Hoa Army Base, Long Binh Army Depot, Bien Hoa Airfield, and the cities of Bien Hoa and Saigon.[1]

---

[1] Bien Hoa is actually pronounced "Ben Wa," and Long Binh like "Long Ben."

I've given many real persons fictitious names. Additionally, I've left several real names as they are. Several quoted conversations are merely an attempt to bring out the essence of words spoken a long time ago and are not necessarily meant to suggest that I have a total and accurate recollection of what was actually said.

My story, I believe, offers the point of view of a very average soldier, his opinions on politics, military frustrations and confusions, and the mass corruption that went on while being stuck in an apparently endless war. It comes out of having kind of been on an up and down emotional roller-coaster ride of sadness, loneliness, laughter, danger, devastation and death. It's the life and times of an ordinary American GI, a two-year stint draftee whose country sent him to war, who became involved in many strange deeds and adventures while engaged in that war, who saw many terrible and terrifying things, and who is finally ready to spit it all out. It's the story of a man who fought his own little war within a war and lived to tell about it.

Memory can be a crowded place. Many more things can happen in one minute of a single soldier's wartime experience than in a novelist's lifetime. And they can happen over and over again. But this tale does not project the typical gung-ho mentality so common among most enlisted soldiers. And, as in so many books, you won't find the blood and guts and shoot-'em-up included herein. Nor the grand strategies, military tactics and secret intelligence. This is a story of common folk, the peons of the military, not the professional commanders, senior officers or high-ranking NCOs.

Advance apologies for any factual errors or omissions. They were unintentional.

Compared to high-ranking officers, NCOs or career soldiers who may be fascinated with military life, or who have had thrilling wartime experiences, my escapades may seem simplistic. Still, I believe that what happened to ordinary, low-ranking soldiers such as myself does have a place in the history of what happened in Vietnam. It's all part of the great experience we call life. That's why I wrote about it. I hope that the private moments, revelations, thoughts and opinions, along with some of the humor you'll find, the dangers I encountered and the anger I experienced, will help you to a greater understanding of what so many of us went through.

If I've accomplished that, my purpose will have been served.

Ivan Lynn Bowman[2]

Judith River Ranch,

Hilger, Montana, 2006

---

[2] Throughout the book my name, Ivan, is used because of standard military procedure. On the other hand, my middle name, Lynn, is often used when the situation pertains to friends or relatives.

WHO'S MY ENEMY?

PROLOGUE

*. . . if you think there's a chance you'll forget,
just stop by The Wall and spend a few minutes
thinking about the people who gave their lives
because their country asked them to.*

FORMER MINNESOTA GOVERNOR JESSE VENTURA

WASHINGTON, DC, JANUARY 1996. THE WALL.

We had run out of film for my still camera. Janet, now
my wife but then a former girlfriend I'd flown to Balti-
more to meet, and who had accompanied me on this
pilgrimage to the National Vietnam Veterans Memorial,
had gone off to a gift shop to buy another roll. As I stood
there searching a thick directory of the Wall for names
of comrades fallen in Nam (including high school buddies) and waiting for Janet to return, I began to slip into
a nervous panic. Recently divorced from my fourth
wife, in the depths of a seemingly endless depression
over both unresolved shit coming out of the war and
a peck of personal troubles – including, obviously, difficulty in creating a good marriage – I began to shiver,
feeling even colder than the already freezing day would
make a person. A strong bout of anxiety was coming on.
I could feel my throat muscles severely tensing up, and
could barely catch my breath.

Where the hell was Janet? She seemed to be taking an
awfully long time. Being alone seemed to increase the

panic. I looked around for help, wondered who I should talk to, who would understand, and what I should say if I did approach some perfect stranger.

Then a thought came to mind: find Janet! I ran in the direction she'd gone, but then eventually stopped, because I had no idea where the gift store was. By now, I was flipping out. Another thought popped into my head: "Take one of your tranquilizers, buddy." Frantically, I searched my pockets for a Xanax. I'd recently acquired the habit of tossing a couple pills into my shirt pocket, but came up empty. My mind in a funk, I'd apparently left them at Janet's place in Mitchelville, near Annapolis.

By now, I was hyperventilating, feeling faint and trembling all over. Maybe I could find a paper bag and breath into that. I'd heard that could help. But where to find a bag?

On the edge of the complete breakdown I was sure was about to overtake me, something said, "Get back to the Wall." So I took off, running again. All the way back my heart raced like a trip-hammer, beating faster and faster. Then, the moment I reached the Wall, a kind of unseen spirit seemed to direct me to place both hands up as high as I could on that endlessly long slab of black granite. Very deliberately, my hands slowly began moving down the cold monolith, my fingertips touching the engraved names, names of the more than 58,000 men and women who had fallen in Vietnam and whose memory would remain forever on this impressive monument.[3]

---

[3] During the Vietnam War sixty-seven American women died or were killed. Eight were military and fifty-nine were civilians. These included Army and Air Force personnel, Red Cross workers, and many who worked for various government agencies. More than 500 WACs were stationed in Vietnam, 600 Air Force women were there, Army, Navy and Air Force nurses and medical specialists numbered over 6000, and large numbers of Red Cross, Special Services, Civil Service, and women in other capacities also served in Vietnam. (Source: Vietnam Women's Memorial Project). Note: Of the 58,000 plus names on the wall, approximately 1300 are still listed as missing.

Slowly, subtly, a gentle warmth began seeping into my fingers. It spread through my hands and arms and down past my neck into my chest. Soon, it enveloped my entire body. Gradually, the immense buildup of tension began to release, and I started feeling slightly safer, more secure. By now, my hands and fingers were so low on the Wall, still crawling over the names, that I found myself kneeling. And noticed that I was breathing almost normally.

Maybe the warmth and safety creeping in had simply been the result of letting go of my own troubles and emotional problems for a time. Maybe it was just thinking about these brave comrades listed on the Wall. Or maybe it was a combination; perhaps they had become a part of me. Whatever it was, I was now starting to sense that I belonged.

I stood up again, gazing down the seemingly forever length of the Wall, scanning the names of all those who didn't make it home. As I waited for Janet to return, my mind drifted back, back to my own arrival in Vietnam, to the experiences I went through during that long and bloody war. I thought of the first day.

CHRISTMAS EVE, 1968. Apparently unaware the cabin intercom was on, the captain of the Pan American 707 cleared his throat. Several of us chuckled. Then he announced, "Welcome to Vietnam. Please buckle your seat belts, we'll be landing momentarily." A long pause, then he added, "Good luck, you guys." By his tone of voice I seemed to detect that the captain might be feeling a bit melancholy about dropping us off in such a dreadfully dismal and lethal place.

Behind me, I heard a deep raspy voice. "Oh yeah! Santa's home, I've got *your* gift, Charlie." Most of us turned around to see who had uttered this wise-ass remark. Turned out to be a buck sergeant, the same lanky, hillbilly-looking dude who had been blasting out "Hound Dog" and "Jailhouse Rock" and "Return to Sender" on his eight-track player ever since we left Oakland, California seventeen hours before. He even wore semi-long, Elvis sideburns. Freaky. As if to rub it in, as the jet continued its decent he deliberately turned up the volume on "Blue Christmas." Shit! Every guy on the plane knew what we were in for. Maybe he was some kind of a sadist, or just a hardcore Army lifer bastard on his second tour of Nam? I'd heard that killing gets into your blood. I glanced at the GI sitting next to me on my right. He showed no emotion; no grin, no smile, not even a tear, as if he didn't give a damn about what he was soon to get into. Toughing it out, I guess. I thought of a card shark playing high stakes poker. But what the hell, I thought, he's an American soldier, just like the rest of us.

The jam packed 707 began to vibrate and whine as it slowed for the landing. As it banked left I got a direct view of the ground. It was nearing midnight, and all I could make out in the pitch-black darkness below were a few scattered lights. Kind of a metaphor for what lay ahead, maybe. So that's Vietnam, I thought; a real inviting landscape! Goodbye California, so long to the "milk and honey" life we left behind. Welcome to Bien Hoa Airfield, Republic of Vietnam.

As I waited in line to disembark down the long stairway that had been rolled out to the jet, an attractive airline hostess winked and offered me a big smile. What a honey. I really needed that.

On the tarmac, a staff sergeant directed us toward the processing center, where we were greeted by a not yet dry behind the ears first lieutenant, who gave us a short welcoming and briefing session. "First rule," he said, "is to do exactly as you're instructed. Charlie's been raising hell in this area lately, and is constantly coming up with new tricks. Those Viet Cong are a damn sneaky bunch."

The briefing finished, we boarded a big green U.S. Army bus that would deliver us to Long Binh Army Base. Except for the motor's hum and the bumps along the road the trip was deathly quiet. Nobody said a word. There was no moon, and in the dark outside each of us could imagine Charlie, lying in wait, as close as our breath.

At Long Binh we retrieved our duffels and were directed by another sergeant to a "hooch," a sort of army barracks. We were issued bedding, assigned a bunk, and warned by the sergeant to "Be quiet, and most definitely don't leave this hooch for any damned thing, because Charlie is all around."

By now, we'd been in South Vietnam for two hours.

As I lay there, a sudden stranger in this war torn and poverty filled land, I wondered what tomorrow would bring. And I was sure my comrades felt the same: a state of shock about our arrival in a place from which we might never return.

We'd been in the hooch for thirty minutes and I was just dozing off when all hell broke loose. The sound of rapid gunfire snapped me awake. Bullets were ripping through the wooden walls. Instinctively, I jumped up, hit the floor and under the bunk I went. Charlie's AK-47 and all kinds of small arms fire continued for a full two minutes. Then, outside we could hear the sound of a huge chopper, the familiar whirling, thump, thump, thump of the blades as it approached. Nervous jitters among us would be an understatement. Through a crack in the hooch's wall we could see its searchlight seeking out the enemy. Then we saw bright white flashes of light and heard two or three bursts of M-60 machine gun fire from the chopper. In minutes, all was quite. I guess this was our "Merry Christmas" from Charlie. We're only a couple hours into this, I thought. What the hell is next? I guess you'd call it some kind of weird shock therapy or mind conditioning. Or maybe a sample introduction to upcoming events. A quick reality check, that's what it was. Since we were all greenhorns to this "war thing," and even though none of us suffered anything worse than jangled nerves, I figured that some damn lifer would have come into the hooch to check on our condition. Nothing at all. Most puzzling.

I had a lot to learn.

In the morning we checked out the bullet holes that had been shot into the hooch. "What happened here last night," I asked the sergeant with the Elvis sideburns.

"You're not dead, are you?" he barked, "*This* is war, punk, so don't ask me about it anymore. Got it?"

What in the hell is wrong with this lifer son-of-a-bitch, I thought to myself. Whose damn side is he on anyhow? Some welcome. I didn't know it then, but in a way this encounter would be typical of my service in Vietnam.

BACK TO 1996. AT THE WALL. Fairly calm now, but with Janet not yet back, I walked along past the thousands and thousands of names, sensing, somehow a new feeling of brotherhood. I thought about brotherhood. About my buddies from Amador High School in Northern California's Sierra foothills, and other comrades I served with who never returned alive. About my own brother, Steve, who served in Vietnam before me, and about what life had been like before I got there myself.

LYNN AND JANET BOWMAN ON THEIR WEDDING DAY
THE MEMORIES, LIKE THE WALL ALWAYS CAST A SHADOW.

WHO'S MY ENEMY?

IT WAS THE BEST OF TIMES . . . IT WAS THE WORST OF TIMES.

BROTHERS AND BEAUTIES

I tell you the past is a bucket of ashes, so live not in your yesterdays, nor just for tomorrow, but in the here and now. Keep moving and forget the post mortems; and remember, no one can get the jump on the future.

CARL SANDBURG

To be in love is merely to be in a state of perpetual anesthesia – to mistake an ordinary young woman for a goddess.

H.L. MENCKEN

JULY 1965. One of the major highlights and a really popular attraction at the annual four-day Amador County Fair was the beauty pageant. As usual, it was held on the opening evening, a Thursday. Ten to fifteen lovely young women usually participated, and I was elated when my brother Steve's longtime high school sweetheart and future wife, the stunningly beautiful tall and blond Sharon Engersol, was crowned Miss Amador County. This made the pageant special for both Sharon's family and mine.

I was twenty-one at the time, and married to my first wife, Sharon Gamble. Oddly, the same first name as Steve's girlfriend. This marriage (mine, not Steve's), coming out of a first, mad passion, had turned out to be a real lemon. We divorced in October 1966. But there was a blessing: I'd fathered a son, Eric. He was about six

1

months old when Sharon and I broke up, and leaving him tore my heart out.

But youth doesn't stand still, does it?

I was soon in love again, with the gorgeous Karen Goodman. We had begun dating in the late months of 1966, taking in high school football games, hanging out and just having fun. I worked for the California Division of Forestry (CDF) then, and was stationed mainly at the small town of River Pines, California, in a place called Pine Lodge Fire Station. My title was Forest Fire Truck Driver (FFTD). Later, the title was renamed Fire Apparatus Engineer (FAE). Because of my unusual three days off and four days on schedule, Karen visited me there quite often.

I recall planting a couple of small Colorado Blue Spruce trees, one on the back lawn near the sidewalk that led from the men's barracks to the fire truck garage and the other on the front lawn between the fire house kitchen and the main county road. Approximately one foot tall when I planted them in the spring of 1966, by the time I went back for a brief visit in 1996 one had become a surprising, magnificent specimen of twenty-five feet; but the other didn't survive the horseplay and football roughhousing among the other CDF workers and firemen that had taken place over the years.

In midsummer 1966, Karen entered the Amador County beauty pageant, the same one my brother's girl-friend had won a year earlier. Although this was only her first attempt to participate, Karen became one of the top three contestants. But when it came to the judging, though she had the looks and the figure she lacked the poise and experience necessary to pass final muster. So, no selection as queen that year. But the following year her best friend urged her to give it another whirl. The friend was sure she'd be a shoe-in. And the friend was right. Nineteen sixty-seven was Karen's year. She hit the jackpot and was chosen queen. I was knocked out that she'd won, and couldn't help bragging about it for the next two weeks.

Soon after that, my life turned completely around.

A letter arrived from my local draft board, ordering me to appear at the Oakland, California Army Induction Center, on November 1, 1967. Since I was divorced from my first wife by now, and unmarried, my military status was 1-A. Finally, I was ripe for the picking.

With me about to leave, and where to, and for who knew how long, Karen and I had a hard decision to make: get married or wait until my return. We were in love, and wanted to take the plunge. But there was a problem: according to gossip we'd heard, a beauty pageant queen wasn't supposed to marry, let alone get pregnant during her yearlong reign. Besides, she had to be available to crown the new queen the following year, and a big-bellied reigning beauty queen, we supposed, wouldn't exactly please the pageant officials–nor the huge crowd of spectators.

Desperately seeking a solution to this dilemma, we went to see Dick Cooper, the Amador County Fair manager, at his home near the small town of Plymouth in California's Shenandoah Valley. By now it was early September, so I still had a couple months before I'd need to report for Army duty. We asked Cooper if it would cast a bad light on Karen, or bend the rules of the county fair board, if we were to marry. He didn't have many answers, so what the hell, we figured–let's do it! We tied the knot on October 15, 1967.

And there was one more reason in my head for getting married: I wasn't about to allow my brother and my father the glory of being the only ones that had hooked up with beauty queens. My brother and I had always looked up to our father, and since he married the finest beauty queen of all, our mother, we needed to show that he didn't have the market to himself. So we carried on with the old macho, manly family tradition, both of us marrying stunning beauties.

My brother and I were very close and had wonderful, loving parents. Steve and I did almost everything together, including fishing, hunting and camping all over the Sierra Nevada. He had chosen me best man at his marriage, and I would definitely have had Steve be my best man, but there was one big problem: he couldn't make it to the wedding because he'd already been drafted, and was serving in South Vietnam with the United States Army.

What really worried my parents and me was that Steve, after his training at California's Fort Ord, had been appointed an infantry Military Occupational Specialty (MOS). In South Vietnam, depending upon your unit and assignment, an infantry (MOS) could get you into one hell of a lot of trouble. Fortunately, Steve ended up as a security guard at Vung Tau Air Base. Hell of a lot better than slogging through the jungle as an infantry grunt.

Vung Tau, located on the shoreline of the South China Sea, was one of the two in-country rest and recreation (R and R) centers. Every serviceman serving in South Vietnam had, by choice, a one-time opportunity for a five-day R and R from active duty. There were ten locations for R and R, but Vung Tau in the south and Cam Ranh Bay farther north were the only in-country locations for serviceman in South Vietnam.

I'd figured the odds of Steve becoming a security guard at an air base were pretty damned slim so it eased my mind a little to find out that he wasn't humping boonies out in some thick-ass jungle crawling with bloodthirsty Viet Cong and NVA troops.

BUT YOUTH DOESN'T STAND STILL, DOES IT?

WHO'S MY ENEMY?

The aim of military training is not just to prepare men for battle, but to make them long for it.

LOUIS SIMPSON, POET

LYNN BOWMAN AT BUNKSIDE, BASIC, FORT LEWIS, WASHINGTON

BASIC

A soldier is a Yahoo hired to kill in cold blood
as many of his own species, who have never
offended him, as possibly he can.

Jonathan Swift, Gulliver's Travels

FORT LEWIS, WASHINGTON. NOVEMBER 1, 1967.

Karen and I had been married just two weeks when I reported for active duty at the Oakland Army Induction Center. And now I found myself in a boot camp platoon, attached to "A" Company, 5th Battalion, 2nd Brigade (A-5-2) for my basic training. Over the next almost two months we went through the normal hell experienced by every recruit: cold-ass rain, endlessly sucking mud, and aching bodies every day until, mercifully, the weather cleared for a much-needed one week break for Christmas.

In the Army there was little chance for give and take about anything. You just followed orders. I vividly remember one particular morning in the barracks. While our tough as nails drill sergeant was conducting a boring monologue covering activities and exercises for the coming week, I suddenly had to sneeze. I quickly covered my mouth in an attempt to muffle the noise. It didn't quite do the job, and I let go with a big Achoo!

The drill sergeant came unglued.

"Bowman, down for twenty pushups," he bawled.

"Sarge, I really didn't mean -- "

"For pissing me off, Bowman, interrupting me and calling me Sarge, you can get down for forty. And I mean right the hell now!"

Well, that shut me up. I immediately dropped to the floor and proceeded with my pushups.

As our sergeant carried on with his one-sided discussion, my platoon "buddy," Private Silva, well out of sight of the staff sergeant, placed his boot in the small of my back, making the pushups twice as hard. I struggled on anyway, without a single peep, while my damned buddy stood there smirking and taunting me.

Entertainment? Well, most evenings we'd gather on the second deck (upper floor) of the barracks to gamble. We started out with penny-ante blackjack, or twenty-one. But since there were rarely any big winners (or losers) we quickly became bored.

Then one bright and inventive character came up with a new and exciting card game. He called it "red-dog" or "in-between." By either handle, this game got the guys really charged up, especially on payday when practically the entire platoon concentrated around the end bunk, either betting on "red-dog" or as enthusiastic spectators. When our first government paychecks were issued, wow! We were all big spenders. Or so it seemed to us back then.

Our drill sergeant had given us strict orders to not gamble during basic training. He'd gone on and on about the various disciplinary actions he and the second lieutenant would dish out, and had made it very clear that if any of us were caught he would come down on the entire platoon. Do you think his lecture had any influence? Let me put it this way: in one ear and out the other. Don't get me wrong; while we respected authority, we were young and slightly rambunctious, red-blooded American soldiers, full of untamed energy. We were lean and mean, we thought, and weren't about to stand by and let a lifer staff sergeant and some young punk butter bar ruin our nightly entertainment.[1] No damn way. So we made sure to always have our eyes peeled, and made sure we had a reliably alert guard at the stairway leading to the upper deck, just in case our tough-ass sergeant or wise guy butter bar decided to pay an unscheduled visit.

Of course, some nights, after a full day of mind games and exhausting exercises, and with mud practically up to our ears, we were just too damn worn out for card games.

One particularly rigorous exercise used "pugil" sticks. Two men were each given a pugil stick – the ends of which resembled crude boxing gloves – and some crazy looking headgear to halfway protect their noggins. The drill sergeant would generally match up two guys of similar size, weight, and physical ability. As each dude squared off, both combatants tried to beat the hell out of each other. And if a recruit didn't make a good showing the drill sergeant came down on him like a son-of-a-bitch. On occasion, however, I was convinced that this dip-shit sergeant deliberately chose combatants of lopsided physical abilities, just to get his whacker off by seeing the stronger guy beat the weaker troop into the ground.

Immediately after this mind-boggling, body-bashing exercise, we were granted a short, desperately needed break. During the break, I looked over and noticed a delivery truck parked near the back door of our mess hall. Why not check it out, I thought. My good friend, Silva (the same guy who had held me down when I

---

[1] Butter bar: second lieutenant. (Because of the single yellow bars on their shoulders.)

endured those forty pushups), came along to see what we could get our hands on. While he kept an eagle eye out for trouble (such as nosy lifers), I scrounged around checking the merchandise. Wasting little time, I snatched a ten-pound box of sliced bacon and another of link sausages. I handed one to Silva, and we both ran like deer back to the barracks.

This had to be our lucky day; we hadn't been spotted. We placed the boxes in the bottom of our gear lockers and prayed we wouldn't have any sudden unscheduled inspections. But now we had a problem: what the hell were we going to do with twenty pounds of raw bacon and sausages? Later that evening, while a game of red-dog was in full swing I told Silva I had an idea.

"Let's go to the latrine," I suggested.

Once there, we stripped off a bunch of paper towels. I dampened several. Then we ducked back to our lockers, picked up our boxes of pork and headed down to the old coal furnace room in the bottom of the barracks. This damned antique furnace was a dinosaur, ancient as the Earth itself. But it worked perfectly for our needs. We cleaned off a large section on top of the old furnace with the paper towels, and unbelievably, were able to stoke up the coal and maintain a perfect temperature while we cooked up the entire stash of pork. Every fifteen minutes or so, Silva or I would trot back into the barracks to deliver up a slug of decently cooked bacon and sausage links for our buddies. Silva and I were proud as peacocks; we'd pulled it off and hadn't been caught.

By the end of our pork cook off Silva and I had practically depleted the latrine paper towel supply to absorb and clean up all the grease. We even had to resort to a half dozen rolls of toilet paper to finish dealing with the mess. Pig grease had been running all over the place, and we sure as hell didn't want to leave any incriminating evidence for our snoopy-nosed drill sergeant. All the evidence, all the grease-soaked paper towels and toilet paper, went right into the old dinosaur furnace and up in smoke.

That was one crazy, fun-filled evening: playing cards half the night, howling at the moon, and dining high off the hog. One of my most memorable and pleasant red-dog nights at the old platoon barracks in Fort Lewis, Washington.

One crucial part of my basic at Fort Lewis, was qualifying with the Government Issue M-14 rifle. The M-14 rifle is a thirty caliber, similar to the conventional 308-caliber rifle. During training, through some serious scuttlebutt, I had heard that if you qualified as an "expert" with the M-14, you'd have a much greater chance of going infantry. Rumor also had it that if you received a "military occupational specialty" (MOS) as an infantryman and you ended up in Vietnam, your chances of leaving there alive were damned slim. That's the situation my brother Steve had first found himself in, before he become a security guard.

Since I had always considered that my chances of ending up in Vietnam were just about guaranteed, I decided that when rifle qualification day came around, I would discreetly (and deliberately) try to miss enough targets at the field range to completely knock me out of the "expert" classification.

My only problem was that I had always enjoyed the hunting and shooting sports. So, by the day the M-14 qualification rolled around, in the excitement of shooting I had completely forgotten about my sneaky plan. Three quarters of the way through the exercise, I had already hit, with ease, and at all ranges and shooting positions, all but one of the silhouette targets. By the time I recognized my stupid forgetfulness I had a real dilemma. I'd have to miss a bunch of targets in order to get my stupid ass out of the "expert" class.

I'd screwed up, big-time. Damn it!

To add to the misery, I'd been having so much fun that I'd completely forgotten that before I'd started the qualification firing the gunny sergeant had distinctly brought it to my attention that the 500-meter range target was electronically malfunctioning and would only pop up about halfway.

"It'll be okay with me if you want to pass it up," he said.

Hell, no, I had thought at the time. It was an irresistible challenge. Every time that half-ass maverick target came up, I'd nailed it fair and square; three times out of three. (I guess you could call me a straight shooter; son of a gun!) But now, I didn't want to raise the suspicion of the "tally and gunny" sergeant and miss the obviously easy or close targets.[2] So how the hell was I going to pull this crazy thing off, and miss enough without looking conspicuous?

Though I felt sort of stupid, just about every time one of the automatic pop-up targets came up beyond 100 meters, I'd put the rifle sights right on the middle of it then discretely and gently pull slightly to the left or right, fire, and miss. Oops! After three or four of these misses my gunny sergeant shouted, "What in the hell are you doing, Bowman? You were well on your way to breaking a range record." Then he came over close and asked, "Are you feeling OK, Bowman? You sick? Feeling dizzy?"

I assured him I wasn't.

Finally, the M-14 qualification was complete. The gunny sergeant began tallying my scores, hits and misses. I began to sweat. Had I missed enough targets?

2 Tally and "gunny" (gunnery) sergeant.

Then the sergeant turned to me and said, "Bowman, you son-of-a-bitch. Nobody, I mean absolutely nobody, has hit that bastard misfit target out there at the 500-meter mark like you. And then you go and miss these damned easy targets. You really piss me the hell off!

You were well on your way to an almost perfect score, and quite possibly an all time range record. Then you blew it to hell in a hand basket. Damn it, Bowman, I could've gotten you on the instructional and shooting team up here at Lewis!"

I didn't know what to say, so I kept my mouth shut.

The sergeant said, "I've got your sad-ass tally, Bowman. What chicken-shit shooting category do ya think y're qualified for?"

"I - I really don't know, Sergeant," I replied.

"You qualified as a damned expert, Bowman!"

"What? Are you sure of the count, Sergeant?"

"Are you disappointed or something? You actually had four more targets to spare," he snapped back.

"Oh, no, Sergeant, that's just great," I said, feeling like an absolute idiot.

I'd missed all of those targets for absolutely nothing. Because I'd ended up as an expert anyway. And if I'd been true to myself and not tried to pull a fast one I might have avoided Nam altogether.

The only remaining question was, would I go infantry MOS or not?

THAT'S ME, NO SHIRT. WITH BUDDIES CUTTING UP IN LATRINE. INNOCENT YOUTH, IN FOR A RUDE AWAKENING

WHO'S MY ENEMY?

POETIC JUSTICE

Women are like elephants to me. I like to look at them, but I wouldn't want to own one.

W.C. FIELDS

Sometimes I wonder if men and women really suit each other. Perhaps they should live next door and just visit now and then.

KATHARINE HEPBURN

AFTER BASIC TRAINING and a few days' leave, I was sent to Fort Hood, Texas for my stateside duty. There, I received a heavy-duty truck driver's MOS designation, a 64B20 within the 2nd Armored – commonly known as the "Hell on Wheels" Division, a tough, rough and ready outfit.

At least one of my worst fears was over. No more worries about the infantry MOS.

But since driving didn't exactly cut it, I began snooping around for other job openings – and found out that the motor pool desperately needed a battalion maintenance clerk. This was a complicated record-keeping job, preparing what was called the "equipment readiness report." Although the last real typing experience I'd had was in my junior year in high school, and even though I'd never got beyond thirty words a minute, my rapid fire bullshitting convinced Captain Murphy, commanding the motor pool, that I could handle this somewhat complicated job.

But even though I'd pulled the wool over his eyes a bit, I was determined to give it my all, prove myself worthy of the clerical work. So what if I was as slow as molasses in January? I decided to follow the advice of my old military style high school typing teacher, Mr. Frank Kane, who used to say, "It's no use cutting a fat hog by slamming on your keys for more words per minute just to make more mistakes." In his book, accuracy was everything.

Granted, my typing skills – which never reached the super speed of Nesta Allen, one of the gals in Mr. Kane's class – were rusty and my speed was somewhere between a tortoise and a lame hare, but I was accurate. So, recalling the "Less yap, more tap" sign in Mr. Kane's class, I got the job done with no hassle, and my "equipment readiness reports" provided essential information for the Department of Defense; the Pentagon. Which puffed me up a bit, because this was quite a responsibility for a PFC (private first class).

After a few weeks of settling in, Captain Murphy asked if I'd like to spruce up my typing skills. This was no order, just a persuasive suggestion, but I figured I'd better take heed and attend the Division typing class. Then too, there was the added incentive of getting a second MOS added to my army records, a 71B20 clerk typist order – which, I figured, might help keep me out of serious trouble should I end up in Vietnam.

So, more typing, until I became pretty good at it.

Until my new wife, Karen, was able to join me, I bunked on the base and we wrote back and forth. But when she did come we rented a small house off the post in the small town of Copperas Cove, Texas. Her arrival was one happy and exciting day, and my lovemaking was especially passionate. "Where the heck did you learn *that* from?" Karen demanded. "Have you been cheating on me?"

"I just picked up some interesting tips from guys at the base," I told her, honestly (since I hadn't been cheating).

She quickly calmed down and we soon settled into a happy married routine.

Except that my army pay wasn't enough to feed a starving mouse; so for extra income, Karen hired on at a hardware store at Killeen, Texas. And me? Well, having played a lot of baseball in Little League and in high school – I maintained a 400 plus batting average all four years and in my junior year had an earned run average (ERA) of 0.00 for the entire season and later even played some semipro ball with the California/Mexican League in Stockton, and had been scouted for pitching by the Cincinnati Reds at Lawrence Park in Lodi, California – I decided to start coaching a Babe Ruth League baseball team on my days off.

APRIL 1968. America was in turmoil. Dr. Martin Luther King had been assassinated. So-called race riots and chaos were raging in many parts of the nation and there was even an increase in unrest among the black and white troops at Fort Hood.

Then, a couple of months later, my radio clock alarm went off. Six-fifteen sharp, as usual. But as I struggled to wake up on that particular morning I heard a lot of excited talk and yelling over the airwaves. The tone of the voices told me something was very wrong, and vague words indicated that an important person or celebrity had been shot. While I dressed in my army uniform, I reached over and turned up the volume. Robert Kennedy had been shot at the Ambassador Hotel in Los

Angeles during his quest for the Democratic nomination for the presidency, and a man called Sirhan Sirhan had been apprehended as a major suspect. So soon after Dr. King's murder, it seemed like the turmoil would just go on and on.

But not all the drama was on the national scene.

"What do you mean you called the cops?" I demanded of my wife, Karen, when she told me what she'd done.

"She stole my treasured wristwatch," said Karen. "I know Ann took it."

"How do you know?"

"I just do. It was here, they visited the other day, and now it's gone."

"Maybe you just mislaid it."

"I didn't mislay it, I looked around and it's not here."

I was livid. Karen, it turned out, had called the Copperas Cove Police Department on the wife of a neighbor; a buck sergeant named David Webster, also stationed at Fort Hood, and accused her of stealing her valuable heirloom wristwatch. The cops had arrived and hauled the wife, Ann, off to jail. And there she stayed. For three days! This pissed me off royally, because the Websters were good friends. And it pissed me off even more when, a week later, Karen found the watch – inside our home. She had mislaid it. Took a while for me to get over that one, because Karen stubbornly refused to even apologize to our good neighbors. And following this incident they cut us off completely. (Who could blame them?)[1]

But life sometimes has a way of evening things out, doesn't it?

---

[1] Sergeant Webster's wife filed suit against Karn and me over this. The judgement went against us and we had to come up with $200 for "actual damages."

In late July 1968 I got some Army leave, and Karen and I flew home to Northern California to attend the Amador County Fair. She was, after all, still the beauty pageant's reigning queen from the previous year, and as such was scheduled to crown her successor. But guess what? Karen was nearly seven months pregnant with our first child! Now wouldn't that be a site to behold, the 1967 reigning queen poached out like a fat deer tick, strutting around on the stage in front of three thousand people? And the pageant rules wouldn't permit it.

Consequently, we sat in the crowded grandstands with Karen's parents and listened as the master of ceremonies announced over the crackling microphone that, "Due to unforeseen" circumstances the reigning queen, Karen Goodman will not be present tonight to crown the new queen. The crowning will be done by Miss Marsha Stone, the 1967 first runner-up."

As all this took place, Karen was sobbing, balling like a baby. It even brought a few tears to my eyes. Even though I was still smarting over the "stolen" watch fiasco, I admit to having felt a bit sorry for my wife.

Still, on the plane back to Fort Hood I was thinking that maybe the anguish Karen went through over the beauty pageant was a fair punishment for putting our good neighbors back in Copperas Cove through such miserable hell over the misplaced heirloom watch.

THAT'S ME, READY FOR MY BATTALION MAINTENEANCE CLERK JOB AT MOTORPOOL.

WHO'S MY ENEMY?

MR. HONKY

The draft is white people sending black people to fight yellow people to protect the country they stole from the red people.

FROM HAIR, THE MOVIE

ONE EARLY MORNING at Fort Hood, just after "police call," Major Campbell had our entire company fall out for a special briefing. What the hell was this all about, we wondered. Well, we found out soon enough. Several companies, including ours, had been chosen for "race riot" duty.

"The purpose of the briefing," said the major, "Is to inform you guys to be prepared to ship out on twenty-four hour notice if the call comes down from Divisional Headquarters, 2nd Armored Division."

This clearly meant that if a "race riot" broke out, we could be shipped anywhere in the country. Then he told us to "Prepare a duffel bag, completely ready with personal items, work uniforms, underwear, and so on. And by no means pack any civvies. I want you boys to drop your cocks and grab your socks. And definitely leave all your damn girly magazines behind!"

We were told that if the call came we'd be issued M-16 or M-14 rifles, plus riot gear and flak jackets. "Also," he went on, "None of you married guys living off base will get out of this riot assignment. No damned excuses!"

And after all that, wouldn't you know it; the call from

divisional headquarters to fall out for riot duty never came.

There did, however, while I was at Fort Hood, seem to be a fair amount of tension and resentment from time to time among many of the black and white troops. In fact, I had a couple small altercations with black dudes. Nothing to write home about, but it did get a bit annoying, and sometimes even hairy.

One particular S.O.B. I worked with in the tool room at the motor pool was a real smart-ass. He constantly bugged me while I worked, and kept calling me "Mr. Honky." I guess he figured he could bully me around. Along with the "Mr. Honky" shit, he'd sometimes semi-threaten to "Kick your ass." For a while, even though it jerked my chain, I let it slide. But eventually it got out of hand. Now, I'm generally an easygoing sort of a guy, but on one particular day my temper got the best of me.

"Okay, you son-of-a-bitch," I said, after he'd made some especially nasty remark,

"You've been on my back too damned long with that blabbermouth of yours! Let's get it on. Let's see how tough you really are. Let's go out behind the conex containers and see if your smart black-ass is as good as my white honky ass."

As we started out of the tool room, walking towards the containers, the bastard all of a sudden stopped and said, "Bowman, I'm really sorry if I've offended you. I really didn't think you'd wanna kick my ass."

"Look, here," I shot back, "I don't mind a little joking around once in a while, but I don't need the kind of smart mouth bullshit you've been dishing out. And don't ever start up that "white honky" crap again, or both of us are going right out behind those containers. And next time, I'm gonna mean business!"

Each morning all of the troops, before they fell out
to their assigned jobs for the day, had to participate in
"police call" or "policing the area." Me too. Any garbage, litter, cigarette and cigar butts had to be picked
up from roads, sidewalks, parking area and the lawns
around company headquarters. About every tenth soldier carried a large, number ten-size coffee can, called
the "cigarette butt can." When each guy collected enough
trash, butts, or other litter he had to locate one of these
"can men" and deposit what he'd collected.

Policing the area generally worked pretty well. We
cleaned the place in just a few minutes then fell out
for our normal duty assignments. But on one particular morning during our regular "police call," as I was
collecting litter, cigarette butts and general trash – and
with my hands fairly full of this crap – I went to drop
my collection into one of the cans. I asked this troop,
a black dude, to stop for a second so I could dump
my collection into his butt can. But he ignored me and
kept on walking. I started after him again. Once again
he completely ignored me and walked off. By the third
time, I got tired of chasing this dip-shit, with my hands
stuffed full of litter, so I ran up close, got in his face and
said, "Stop, damnit!"

"I'm not your damned nigger, Whitey," he said, "So
bug the hell off!"

Then he shoved me, almost knocked me down. Well,
that did it. I was in no mood to stand there with my
hands full of junk and have a polite sociological discussion about racial issues. I just wanted the dude to take
my garbage so I could move on. Disgusted, I dropped
the collection of crap at his feet then opened my right
hand and slapped the sucker upside the top of his head.
As his army cap fell to the ground, I turned on my heel
and walked off.

I had nothing special against the black troops, and in fact a couple of my good buddies were black. But this dude had a total lack of respect for a fellow GI. To be charitable, maybe he had a brain fade, or was just having a bad day. Too bad, I thought, because we all had one goal and one mission: get through our tour of duty and move on. I guess it was just a sign of the times.

And I'm sure as hell glad our company never got called out for riot duty.

LYNN, FELLOW TROOP AND WINO (RIGHT)

"WE ALL HAD ONE GOAL AND ONE MISSION: GET THROUGH
OUR TOUR OF DUTY AND MOVE ON."

We should declare war on North Vietnam. . . We could pave the whole country and put parking strips on it and still be home by Christmas.

RONALD REAGAN, 1965

Yeah, come on all of you, big strong men,

Uncle Sam needs your help again.

He's got himself in a terrible jam

Way down yonder in Vietnam

So put down your books and pick up a gun,

We're gonna have a whole lotta fun.

"I-feel-like-I'm-Fixin'-To-Die"

COUNTRY JOE McDONALD

THE VIETNAM SHUFFLE

*We are not going to send American boys nine
or ten thousand miles from home to do what
Asian boys should be doing for themselves.*

PRESIDENT LYNDON B. JOHNSON, OCTOBER 1964

OCTOBER 1968. Preliminary orders had arrived. I was soon to be shipped out. . . to Vietnam. Soon after, a troop returning from there to finish his stateside duty was ordered to replace me at my motor pool clerk's job. Captain Murphy was surely aware that I was soon to ship out, so he must have figured he might as well give my slot to a deserving veteran. I was shifted to the adjacent battalion tool room for typing and record keeping, a job similar to my other clerk's position – except that some of the troops in the tool room were hard to get along with. Also, I was now placed back on the roster for extra duties such as kitchen police (KP), police call (PC), and guard duty (GD).

The Vietnam troop who took over my motor pool position outranked me, but since he acted like such a know-it-all smart ass, I resented letting him have my cushy clerks job. However that soon backfired on him. He couldn't seem to get the battalion equipment readiness report done correctly or on time and his paperwork was stacking up day by day.

Both he and Captain Murphy had treated me like a pile of dog shit over the whole job change, but now they were up against the wall trying to get paperwork out,

27

and needed my assistance. Which seemed kind of ironic, because if he hadn't been such a smug know-it-all, or even if he'd showed me some kind of respect and had the balls to ask me, I'd gladly have helped to bail him out. What the hell, you find all kinds in the Army just like everywhere in life, and you do the best you can.

And anyhow, I had a bigger worry: Vietnam.

On the evening news on Karen's and my small TV at home, protesters were marching in the streets and congregating in city parks all over America. And even many of our returning Vietnam vets were joining the crusade to end the war.

Emotionally, I was stuck somewhere between a patriot and a protester. Did I really want to find myself slogging through the rice paddies and jungles of Vietnam, and maybe die for absolutely nothing? General William (Westy) Westmoreland was demanding more and more troops, and the number of American casualties mounted daily. It suddenly seemed to me as if the war served no real purpose other than killing off young Americans by the thousands. And the morale of the troops here at Fort Hood kept diminishing as the war rolled relentlessly on. Emotionally, I was all mixed up (to say the least).

We all wanted to believe in our president and our military intelligence, but had reservations about our involvement in Vietnam. Like most of my comrades I was both honored and proud to be an American serviceman and was ready to serve a just cause; but something was missing, something we couldn't quite put our finger on. We couldn't find the last piece of the puzzle that would make our sacrifice worthwhile.

I began to analyze myself. Here I was, a strapping six-foot three inches, weighing slightly over 200 pounds and in damn good shape compared to the average troop.

Besides my baseball prowess, I'd been a high school track star. I'd broken school records in both B and A Division high hurdles, and had long-jumped almost twenty-one feet. I'd also high-jumped nearly six and a half feet (in the old "scissors" style). The All-American boy.

And yet, when it came to the war in Vietnam, I felt like some kind of a chickenshit coward. I feared the unknown. I feared death. Was I normal, I asked myself? Were other troops as scared shitless of war as I was, or was it just me? Karen was expecting a baby soon so there was that concern too. What the hell did all of this really mean? In the end, the only satisfactory answer I could come up with was that I was a red-blooded American serviceman who had his fears and doubts. And if any GI didn't have some fear of war, I told myself, then there was probably a screw loose inside his damn head.

Shortly after receiving the depressing news that I was going to be sent to Vietnam, I started snooping around, talking to my fellow troops to find out who was responsible for making out the shipping orders. And I discovered that the guy whose good side I needed to get on was Specialist Frederick Freeman, the clerk in charge of the Special Leaves and Orders Department.

Since I couldn't stand a chance of getting busted, I had to be extremely careful in making my approach. But I was lucky. Fred was a damned straight shooter, and once I'd wormed my way in he and I actually became good friends. Fred was a fellow Californian, and he and his wife Rita started getting together with Karen and me on our days off. With our newfound friendship, I soon felt confident enough to start discussing him delaying (or detouring) my posting to Vietnam. He agreed to hold up the orders as long as he possibly could, but couldn't guarantee that I wouldn't end up there sooner or later.

The normal tour of duty for a GI in Vietnam was twelve months. And by now I had less than a year left in the army, so each and every day that Fred procrastinated with the shipping orders, I'd have less time to serve if I did get shipped out. And yes, I did mull this posting to Vietnam over and over, even in my dreams.

But Fred warned that the talk in his office wasn't optimistic. He'd snooped around one morning and had overheard a conversation between two young junior officers. They'd said that troop body counts were mounting by leaps and bounds. And the Army was despicably thinking about lowering intellectual standards for new officers because they were also dying off like sick flies, so replacements were desperately needed.[1]

"It sounds like a damn death trap over there," Fred burst out with a worried look on his usually cheerful face, "Especially for the front liners and the grunts. And with your primary MOS of a 64-B20, you won't be much better off, Bowman. You'll probably end up driving those heavy-duty trucks somewhere in the middle of a thick-ass enemy infested jungle. So if I delay your shipping orders for a few days, big damned deal."

As it happened, I noticed my name on the top of the orders list on the chalkboard just inside First Sergeant Davis' "Tops" office inside company headquarters. Each day as I walked down the long hallway to work, I glanced anxiously at the names on the chalkboard. Although my name was right up there, days kept slipping by without hearing any bad news. Then one morn-

---

[1] Between 1966 and 1967, Officer Candidate School officer production at six branches (Benning, Belvoir, Sill, McClellan, Gordon, and Knox) jumped from 3,881 to 18,334 men and WACs. An almost fifty percent attrition rate that attended classes in the peacetime years had dropped to, at maximum, five percent. The running joke at Benning was that the "standards of OCS haven't been lowered, it's just that the students aren't required to meet them anymore."

ing I noticed a check mark and a big white circle around my name. Fingernail biting time! That evening after work I told Fred about the changes on the chalkboard, and also mentioned that he'd probably hear some shit come down from the brass at my company headquarters.

Fred was cool. "Bowman, just hang on," he smiled, "I've got it totally under control." But that didn't calm me down. "We're doomed," I thought, "We're gonna get the shaft, we're both going to the big house over this damned deal!"

Over the next few days I practically lived at the chalkboard in the hallway. One particular morning, First Sergeant Davis and Major Campbell were both standing directly in front of it, chatting. The sergeant had a stick pointer, and was pointing it directly at my name. I paused discreetly for a few seconds at the half open door of the "Top's" office and listened intently.

"That tall slim blond guy, the tool room clerk down at the motor pool, PFC Bowman, has been on top of this board for at least twelve to fifteen days too long," said First Sergeant Davis, "I wonder where the hell his damned shipping orders have gone. The other troops seem to be getting theirs on a timely and regular basis."

So as not to get my ass in a sling for eavesdropping, I beat feet and made a hasty retreat, and after duty that evening went to warn Fred of this latest development. Fred told me that two MP's and an officer had just been into his office, asking why my shipping orders for Vietnam hadn't been cut and sent out. Fred, a real talker (he could sell snow to Eskimos), told me he had let loose with a flurry of words, bamboozling them with a string of bullshit excuses.

But I sensed that the time was getting near, and I was ready to throw in the towel and call it quits.

"Damn it Bowman," he said, "Don't get impatient. I've still got it all under control." Fred chuckled and tapped the side of his nose with his finger. "There's a right way, a wrong way, the Army way – and my way. Just hang in there."

Karen, who was nearly eight months along with our baby by now, said she couldn't keep her mind on her work after she'd heard that it wouldn't be long before I was shipped out. So she quit her job at the hardware store in Killeen.

But one of my friends, a cook at the company mess hall, had a more positive reaction. "Hey, Bowman," he said, "Let's have one final celebration, one big shindig." So on our next day off my friends and I got loaded on beer, and my buddy the cook got the bright idea to raid the company mess hall. He had key access to the back door of the kitchen. At about 2400 hours (midnight) I drove my trusty 1965 Ford pickup – called "The Beamer" for the twin I-beam suspension – around to the back door of the mess hall kitchen. Once there, we were like kids in a candy store; we loaded up everything we could lay our hands on. It was almost a miracle that the MP's didn't catch us and nail our asses to the wall. We had a great party and the food left over came in handy because Karen and I had been having a bit of a cash flow problem since she'd quit her job.

Time kept slipping away. And no shipping orders.

Then, one day down at the motor pool, I was presented with a note ordering me to appear at First Sergeant Davis' office, ASAP. Nail biting time again! This was it, I figured. My orders had certainly come. Or else I'd been caught with my pants down, trying to arrange this heavy-duty conspiracy to delay the orders. Shaking inside, I headed straight for Davis' office.

Without even a quick hello, the sergeant pointed a bony index finger and told me to report to Major Campbell's office next door. Which I promptly did.

Campbell, the company commander, asked if I knew of any logical reason why I hadn't received my orders yet.

"No, sir," I said, standing smartly at attention and looking as innocent and uncomprehending as I could, "I have no idea where the orders are, sir."

"Sometimes there are delays of a week or two, but not four goddamned weeks or more!" he snapped back. "I'll be checking into the matter without delay. Someone's going to get hung out to dry for this, Bowman. Take my word."

That evening after work I told Fred what had transpired. Fred was still cool as a cucumber. "Well, Bowman," he said, "We won't be able to hold out much longer. But I'm working on another angle." He must have had his ass well covered, I thought. (The man was strong-willed and had gobs of courage.)

The next day, almost as I'd expected, the same two MP's – but with two young officers along this time – appeared at Fred's desk. He pretended not to notice them and continued with his paperwork. Then one of the MP's hit the desktop with a nightstick. Wham! Fred looked up, somewhat startled.

"If PFC Bowman's shipping orders for Vietnam aren't on Major Campbell's desk by tomorrow," said the baton-wielding MP as he leaned over Fred's desk with a menacing glare, "Like pronto, bright and early, all hell's gonna break loose in this office."

"And there could be several Article 15s and possibly a court-martial. Do you fully comprehend that, Specialist Freeman?" added one of the officers for good measure.

"Yes sir, I'll get right on those orders, sir," Fred answered, knowing he was beaten.

Well almost.

That evening, Fred phoned to tell me he had no alternative but to make out the orders ASAP. But since he'd already given me the maximum allowable amount of leave time before shipping out from Fort Hood, he was smart enough to know he could write up an emergency leave because by now Karen was due to have the baby any day. He also advised me that if Karen had the baby before I was shipped to Vietnam, I might be able to get an additional special emergency leave drawn up and processed through the Red Cross back in Northern California.

In terms of delaying tactics and high-class bullshit, Fred knew every ploy. And he had one more slick idea up his sleeve. "When you report to Oakland Army Center in Northern California to ship out to South Vietnam," he said, "You can stall for a few more days by going to a 'psycho doctor' on the base. I'm sure that you have the ability to come off as a bit nutso, right?"

"Sure, I think so," I replied.

"And remember, Bowman," he went on, "Each and every day you drag out the shipping process at Oakland will be less time you have to serve in Vietnam, and that might be the one damned thing that saves your ass."

NOVEMBER 18, 1968. Karen gave birth to our daughter, Carrie. Then, remembering what Fred had told me, I got a special extension leave through the Red Cross. But the inevitable and dreadfully feared day finally came, and I reported to the Oakland Army Center, ready to ship out.

While waiting at the Center, I called Karen and asked if she'd come down for a visit, since I was eager to see her one more time before I left. For all we knew this might be the last time we'd see one another. Though she agreed, she also seemed strangely reluctant.

While she was with me we made love (if you can even call it that) in the back end of a large, vacant barracks. And though I tried to get her to stay a bit longer, it seemed as if she couldn't wait to head for home. In fact, during the entire visit she gave me the distinct impression that her mind was preoccupied. I began to think the unthinkable: had Karen found a man to replace me? We'd only been apart for a couple days, so how could she think of doing such a thing? Especially now! Even though I tried not to let this get under my skin, I couldn't let it go. She'd never treated me like this before. What the hell was she up to?

Meanwhile, I still kept trying to get out of Vietnam. Or at least stall the departure a bit longer. With Fred's final words front and center, I eventually got an appointment with a doctor at the mental ward, a top-notch "psycho quack," as I thought of him. Tossing bullshit right and left, I told him about the new baby and that my wife desperately needed me at home to help out. For good measure, I let him know that I'd been all "nerved up" and had been having major dizzy spells.

Clearly unimpressed, the doc told me I'd have to ship out, "And if your nervous condition and dizziness flares up and your home problems get out of hand, you can always see a doctor in Vietnam. If the military sees fit to send you back home, then that's what they'll do."

As I listened to him ramble on I suddenly got real. Hey Bowman, I said to myself, what the hell *are* you

35

going to do about your home problems way off in Vietnam? Absolutely nothing, I answered myself. You'll be too damn busy keeping your ass out of trouble to worry about anything else. So I gave myself a large mental kick in the butt and decided to ship out just as soon as I could. After our miserable attempt at lovemaking in the back of the barracks, I'm sure that was just fine with Karen too.

I left Travis Air Force Base in a Pan American 707 on Christmas evening, 1968. We landed first in Hawaii, where many of the troops got off the big jet and went for a cold soda or a beer. Thirty minutes or so on the ground, and away we went again. To the Philippines this time. When we got off for a stretch this time, we felt as if we were walking into a furnace. This was our last stop, and then it was on again to our final destination: Bien Hoa Air Base, Republic of Vietnam.

A new life was about to begin.

LYNN BOWMAN, BIEN HOA, 1969

STEVE BOWMAN, VUNG TAU, 1967

VIETNAMESE BOYS STANDING BY MY BUS
SMOKING AMERICAN CIGARETTES.

DRYING ARMY FATIGUES ON CONCERTINA
WIRE - FIREFIGHT IN THE BACKGROUND

JANUARY 1969, PFC IVAN LYNN BOWMAN

THE NEWBY GUY

Youth is the first victim of war; the first fruit of peace. It takes twenty years or more of peace to make a man; it takes only twenty seconds of war to destroy him.

BAUDOUIN I, KING OF BELGIUM (1951-93)

American soldiers. . . don't fight for what some presidents say on TV, they don't fight for mom, apple pie, the American flag. They fight for one another.

COL. HAL MOORE (SEVENTH CALVARY, VIETNAM)

THAT'S ME. THE "NEWBY GUY" as I was called by the men in my hooch. But I'll get to that.

Christmas Morning. Long Binh Army Base, 1968; 0800 hours. Our first daylight in South Vietnam.

"Good morning," said the buck sergeant, a three-striper head cook for the mess hall with his front teeth knocked out and huge potbelly hanging over his belt. He stood there grinning amiably with his hands on his hips as the new recruits walked down through the chow line. To me, he seemed like the kind of guy who, if you asked him "How many donuts are in a baker's dozen?" he'd have been mentally stumped.

But boy, oh boy could he cook! Great chow. We stuffed our gullets with instant scrambled eggs, burnt bacon, grease-soaked fried potatoes, blackened toast and a strong, hot cup of Joe. Then, after our first breakfast in Vietnam, we were told to fall out, get our Army issue duffle bags and get ready for "in processing."

With all our gear crammed into a large olive drab (OD) green army bus, we were transported to the 537th Personnel Service Company at Bien Hoa Army Base, an administrative post within the 1st Logistical Command: III Corps of the Saigon Support Command. During the half hour drive through a lush, green countryside, I looked out on enormous truck gardens and vast rice paddies cross-sectioned with canals, waterways, and dikes. Peasants wearing big white hats, and occasionally aided by a water buffalo or two, were busy working the gardens and paddies. A scene of great peace and beauty. Hard to believe this country was at war; though I naively wondered why there were mesh wire screens on all the bus windows.

At Bien Hoa we were told to grab our gear and get in line. Soon after arriving, each new recruit or replacement troop had to go through this "in processing," a review of our record or military history, in order to place us in the unit we'd be most qualified for. In most cases this depended on our primary MOS (Military Occupation Specialty), but when a position needed to be filled fast a recruit could be assigned to a unit outside of his primary MOS – so long as he had the expertise.

Frightened half to death of my unknown assignment, and picturing myself trying to keep my head down in the middle of some steamy jungle while unseen Viet Cong took potshots at me, I was standing in line along with some forty other recruits. Butterflies rumbling around in my stomach, I stepped up to the window and handed my file to a Warrant Officer named Gilmore.

He scanned the papers, as I began to sweat. Finally, he looked up.

"Bowman," he said, "I see here that you're a heavy duty truck driver."

"Yes, sir."

"Have you ever driven a bus?"

"Yes, sir, I've driven a standard sized student bus for Stockton College in California, and I drove one for a large church group in Northern California, in a small town called Jackson."

"Do you have any proof you're a qualified bus driver?"

I swallowed hard. But then remembered my California driver's license. I grabbed for my wallet, pulled it out and removed the license. On the backside it was stamped, "May drive any bus while holding a valid driver's license." I handed it to Officer Gilmore.

"How'd you like to drive the same bus you boys just arrived on?" he said.

I looked around for a split second, caught the dismayed looks on some of the other guys at the assignments they were probably pulling, and thought that this would surely be better than driving a heavy-duty truck on some muddy back-ass jungle road crawling with Charlies. I jumped at the chance. You might say I was in the right place at the right time. They

needed a replacement driver fast, and because of my previous experience and truck driver's MOS, the warrant officer obviously felt that I had the qualifications. Still, it was surprising (and something of a relief) to be chosen for this plum job from among the thousands of new recruits; driving the same damn bus I rode in on. But when I found out that those mesh-covered windows were to block grenades or other small explosives from blasting into the bus, I figured it wasn't quite time to start licking my chops.

"Where did you say you lived in California?" the warrant officer asked as he filled out the paperwork.

"A small town in Northern California called Pine Grove. East of Sacramento and Stockton on State Highway 88."

He sort of gasped, let loose with a small laugh and said, "That's quite unbelievable. I used to drive through Pine Grove a lot when I lived in Sacramento. Up 88 to go trout fishing and camping at Silver Lake, Bear River Reservoir, and Twin Lakes."[1]

What a small world, I thought! Officer Gilmore was practically from my back yard.

Two busses were assigned to the 537th Personnel Service Company at Bien Hoa, one for myself and the other one for PFC Rory Robinson. The driver I replaced was going home in a few days, so he trained me on all the bus stops I'd be making over at the big Long Binh Army Base. And there were plenty. He also ran me by the 90th Replacement Battalion were I'd be picking up hoards of newly arrived troops. I had only a few days to become familiar with all the stops, and then it would be up to me to transport the new guys to their units. Rory and I worked well as a bus driver team and over time became

---

[1] Twin Lakes was later renamed Caples Lake.

great friends. He was from around Hollywood, so we had something slightly in common – we were both from California. Four hundred miles apart, but in Vietnam that was almost like having a buddy from home.

After first picking up replacement recruits from the 90th and taking them on to "in processing," Rory and I finally let them off back at their assigned duty units at the Long Binh Army Base.[2] But then, once I became familiar with the route, Officer Gilmore told me I'd have to begin picking up the Vietnamese "hooch" (barracks) maids down in Bien Hoa city.

These hooch maids were predominantly young. (Older Vietnamese women we called "mamasans.") I began picking them up with the bus each and every day of the workweek.

Mainly assigned to base hooches, the maids did the cleaning, laundry and making beds. Generally, each group of troops within a hooch chipped in to hire two maids. On average, each maid earned twenty to twenty-five dollars a month. Not exactly a king's ransom, but a hell of a lot of money for a poor peasant in a third-world country like Vietnam. And (who could blame them), some hooch maids were not above the call of "extra duty" if the price was right.

The hooch was home. It was a place to be protected, a place where you watched out for yourself and your buddies. One evening, one of the old, well seasoned hooch hands, Specialist 5th Class Walker, briefed me on the most important rule.

"If you hear any incoming rounds," he said, "mor-

[2] The ten major military units served by the 90th Replacement Battalion within the Long Binh Army Base and surrounding areas were: United States Army, Vietnam, lst Logistical Command, lst Signal Brigade, lst Aviation Brigade, II Field Force, 44th Medical,18th Military Police Brigade,199th Light Infantry Brigade, llth Armored Cavalry Regiment and the 20th Engineer Brigade. All these major units were included within III Corps Tactical Zone of South Vietnam.

tars or rockets that sound like they're not friendly fire, or like they're coming in from a strange direction, be sure to yell 'incoming!' And yell it real loud. At least twice. This will alert the rest of the guys in the hooch that the Charlies are out there playing games again."

"How come?" I asked.

"Because it will alert some of these deadbeats and dimwits to drop their cocks and get the message that they'd better get their asses out of their bunks and get the hell out of here. And if they don't, it's not your damn fault. You did your thing."

He paused to let that sink in. Then, pointing his finger out the open hooch doorway, he added, "After you yell, get your butt out to that sandbagged bunker as fast as you can. And keep your ass down real low!"

"What if I'm asleep and don't hear anything?"

"Then you're a dumb-ass klutz, all cranked out on weed. Or Charlie's already taken you out," he replied, laughing.

"Thanks a lot, Walker," I replied, somewhat sarcastically, "This rather 'enlightening information' ought to let me sleep well tonight."

And this is where the term "newby guy" comes in.[3]

The above conversation occurred while I was still the "new guy" or the "newby guy" as I was called within the hooch. It was a normal thing for every new replacement troop to have to win recognition and respect from his comrades. For a while it was frustrating, but I soon began to be accepted by the guys – at least the ones that

---

[3] I suppose one could say that Richard M. Nixon, inaugurated as America's 37th president in January of 1969, was also a "newby guy." For his swearing in the president-elect had the Bible opened to Isaiah 2:4 – "Nation shall not lift up sword against nation, neither shall they learn war anymore."

really counted. The rest were a lost cause. To hell with them, I decided.

Three of us in the hooch became good friends. We each took a nickname granted to us by what we called the "hooch whorehouse court." And it was a guy's previous background experience that decided how these nicknames got chosen. We were living through a crazy time, of course, so I suppose we did a lot of goofy things to take our minds off the tension and build up our comradeship and morale.

My buddies were some characters! Specialist 4th Class Lucchesi's parents owned a small winery in California's Napa Valley, so he became "Wino." Lucchesi used to tell us about going with his father to look for special varieties of grapes for the old man's wines. His father liked a big glass of Burgundy with his lunch and dinner, and even when Lucchesi Jr. was a young tyke he always let him have a small glass at meals. He especially enjoyed the toasting of wine glasses with his dad, and though he was Italian through and through we thought it more fitting to call him "Wino" instead of "Dago" – a moniker a lot of Italian guys got stuck with.

Specialist 4th Class Garcia grew up in the New York area. He was always bullshitting about being a lover boy and ladies man, and told us that the girls at his high school called him a big flirt and nicknamed him "Frenchie" because of his super-duper French kissing. Even though we thought he was bragging, we gave him the benefit of the doubt and let the name stick.

My nickname went with the bus-driving job but didn't seem to stick as much as Garcia's and Lucchesi's. Depending on their mood, the rest of the troops would call me "Bus Boy" or "Tripper." But that changed.

On January 17, 1969 I was promoted from PFC lst Class to Specialist 4th Class, so a small celebration was in order down at the base club. Now that I'd joined the ranks of the specialists, it was no longer cool for Wino, Frenchie, or the rest of the troops in the hooch to regard me as some dumb-ass peon. So all of a sudden I became "Specialist Ivan Bowman." My real name; sort of had a nice ring to it – so that evening I gladly bought all the beers for Frenchie, Wino and myself.

In my letters home, I wrote about driving the bus, about how many new troops were flooding into Vietnam, about picking up recruits and taking them to their units; and I tried to suggest that in spite of the danger all around, my family didn't have to worry about me.

January 22, 1969

Dear Mom, Dad, and Marc [my little brother],

Nothing much new here, but five Viet Cong were killed out on the Bien Hoa Airport last night. The VC is starting to act up because of this damn post-TET or whatever the hell it is. They don't monkey around here too much though, because they really get their asses shot off by the planes and helicopters. But a few still try…

One evening later that month, hanging out in the hooch after returning from the base club with a few beers under our belts, Frenchie and I scammed up what became one of several crazy stunts. We decided to play a low down trick on Wino, to see if we could get him ticked off.

"Would you mind turning that volume down a bit on that radio of yours, Wino," I said, "I need to have a little chat with you."

"What's up, guys?" he said, leaning over to switch off the radio.

"We know that you're married," I went on, "But did we hear you say something the other day to the effect that you and your wife have one of those young rug-rats at home in California?"

"I sure do. A cute little boy. He's about fifteen months old by now."

Frenchie joined in. "By the way, I'm kind of curious, Wino, do you remember how much your little baby weighed at birth?"

"I sure do. He was a whooping big guy. Almost nine pounds."

Frenchie and I started jumping up and down holding our crotch areas.

"Wow man, that's a real big-ass horse."

Wino looked at us, and thought we'd gone absolutely whacko.

"By the way Wino," I asked, "Did your wife have a normal birth when she had that big-ass kid of yours?"

"What do ya mean by a normal birth, Bowman?"

"I mean, did she have it the normal way – the hard way, right between her legs – like down here or what?"

"Hell, is there any other way?" he asked, puzzled.

"Damn strait, Wino. My wife had hers by Caesarean section," I said. "The delivery doctor cut a hole in her stomach, just big enough to take the kid out. He reached in, grabbed the babe and out it came, just like that. That's all there was to it. Slick as a damned whistle."

Wino said, "No way, my wife didn't have it like that, I'm sure of it. She had it right between her legs."

"Oh, my God!" exclaimed Frenchie, "No wonder you're so damned screwed up all the time. You've got to get with the damn program, Wino!"

"Wait a minute, guys," I said, as I walked over to my bunk area and picked up a cantaloupe that one of the cooks from the mess hall had given me. (The melon was maybe six inches in diameter, a real whopper.) "Look at the size of this melon, Wino. Do you realize the damned pain and damage something this size would create goin' right between your wife's legs?"

"You're right, Tripper," agreed Frenchie, "I'm gonna insist, in fact I'm gonna demand that my wife is gonna have to have one of those Caesarean deals. That's if I ever get the guts to get married and have kids."

"Do you guys really think that's best?" said Wino, acting seriously worried now.

To rub salt in his wound, Frenchie said, "Did you by chance at least have your wife get one of those husband stitch deals when she had the kid?"

"What in the hell is a husband stitch deal?"

"Tell 'em, Frenchie," I said.

"Well, the 'uptight doctor' takes up an extra stitch or two to tighten things up down there after a melon sized kid stretches things all out of whack. Do you fully understand what I'm saying here?"

"Uh . . . Yeah, I think so."

Frenchie was standing there with the big melon pinched between his inner thighs as he added, "Just imagine the damage this would do to a woman. If I ever get married, my gal's gonna be uptight and out of sight! That must be where the U.S. Army came up with their name for their quarterly magazine, 'Uptight.' " Then he continued with, "Well, being as your wife didn't get either one of those Caesarian deals or a 'husband's stitch,' you really won't have to worry about her screwing and cheating around on you. Once those damned grease-ball hippies, dopers, long hairs and crazy war protesters in California find out that she's as loose as a goose because of her major malfunction at the junction, they won't touch her with a ten-foot-pole. So think positive, Wino, maybe there's a good side to all this."

Finally, Wino cracked, got all pissed and shouted, "To hell with you guys!"

Frenchie and I went over and grabbed him and hugged him a bit and I said, "Come on boy, we're jackin' you around. Messin' with your head. Here, have another beer, just forget it!"

As Wino stood there steaming, Frenchie and I walked off to get another piss-warm beer.

"We'd better offer something more than that poor excuse for an apology, don't ya think?" said Frenchie, "We probably took this damned thing way too far. He thought we were serious, Bowman. We don't need him gettin' all down in the dumps because of our stupid bullshit."

With our beers in hand, and our tails a bit between our legs, we went back and told Wino we'd been shining him on and it was all bullshit, and we hoped he'd forget it. He looked at us hard for a long moment then we all burst out laughing. Then we each retired to our bunks for the rest of the evening, with Wino's forgiveness having been granted. (At least it seemed like it was.)

So much for the foolish junior high school level of horseplay that goes on when a lot of what's on your mind is about maybe getting killed the next day. The war was a bond, so comradeship became doubly important.

FEBRUARY 2, 1969. GROUNDHOG DAY. I'd been in Vietnam just over a month. We never heard if the groundhog actually did see his shadow this year, but I did know one thing for sure: it was my birthday. This particular birthday, I had twenty-five new troops to deliver to various units in Long Binh. I made all of my stops and had a little extra time left over, so I went to the PX (Post Exchange) in Long Binh and picked up a few goodies and some booze for my small party that evening in the hooch.

Since Frenchie was from New York, it seemed appropriate when I located some New York Champagne, so I went to the PX to purchase several bottles. I was actually surprised to find quality Champagne there. And at less then three bucks a bottle the price was a bargain. I picked up a case of Falstaff Beer too, just in case some of the others in the hooch wanted to join in. And for Wino, who obviously liked wine, I located a nice bottle of red Burgundy.

By the time I got back to the hooch, Wino and Frenchie were at Frenchie's bunk area, just bullshitting and waiting for me.

"It's about damned time," said Frenchie, "We thought the Charlies must have caught your ass in the dark around Cong Paddies." (The rice paddies where the Viet Cong regularly hung out.)

"Thanks a lot guys, you sure don't have much faith in me!" I said, "Well, anyway, let the party begin!"

A few of the other troops came over for a couple of quick beers, then Frenchie, Wino, and I got down to serious partying. They sang me "Happy Birthday," and I got to blow out two candles, one on a cupcake that Frenchie got from the mess hall kitchen and the other on the top of a Falstaff Beer can that Wino had made up. We popped the corks on the Champaign, and drank and sang and carried on like the three cutups we were.

Frenchie had snookered some poor troop out of his treasured 45-rpm record player, but said he'd won it fair and square in a cribbage game. With his bragging, I wondered if he was giving us the full skinny.

When we played a record with a tune we knew pretty well, we'd raise our bottles of Champagne and play like they were microphones. We chimed in with "Devil or Angel" and "Take Good Care of My Baby," by Bobby Vee, "Teenager In Love," by Dion and the Belmonts, "Diana," by Paul Anka, "Dream Lover," by Bobby Darin, "Calendar Girl," by Neil Sedaka, "Mr. Lonely," by Bobby Vinton, and "My Special Angel," by Bobby Helms.

By the time we killed the Champagne we'd drank so much we couldn't even stand, let alone carry a tune. So we fell back on Frenchie's bunk and listened to music on the military radio station. Later, after goofing off a while longer, we staggered off to our respective bunks. Wino practically crawled to his. I had the furthest to go, because mine was near the end of the hooch. But a hell of a lot closer to that lifesaving sand-bunker.

Which would come in handy, because all hell was about to break loose.

SPEC-4 BOWMAN, ON BUNK IN HOOCH

WHO'S MY ENEMY?

THE SCENE WAS ONE OF COMPLETE CARNAGE: A DEVASTATED VILLAGE LYING
ON THE OUTSKIRTS OF BIEN HOA CITY, AND VERY NEAR OUR ARMY BASE

POST-TET / 1969

We had to destroy the village in order to save it.

AMERICAN MILITARY PRESS OFFICER IN VIETNAM

Violence is the universal objective law of all thorough national liberation revolutions.

NORTH VIETNAMESE GENERAL VO NGUYEN GIAP

DURING THE WAR we got all kinds of news reports and heard talk about four-star General Vo Nguyen Giap, head of the North Vietnamese Army. The guy was apparently some kind of military genius. We heard that more than forty years before, he'd run the French out of Indochina. And in 1968, just a year before I got there, he'd launched the TET (lunar New Year) offensive. The combined North Vietnamese Army (NVA) and Viet Cong (VC) forces had attacked simultaneously all over the damn country. Even invaded the U.S. Embassy in Saigon. And this was after our military was telling the world the VC and NVA was on the ropes.

Well, in late February of 1969 Giap was still at it. Though not quite as intense or as well organized as the TET offensive had been, for several days and nights the VC and NVA troops combined forces to make several very aggressive assaults in an attempt to penetrate our army base at Bien Hoa. They also staged a courageous offensive against Bien Hoa Air Base.

This was all part of Giap's strategy. The NVA and VC knew full well that by attacking big American bases such as those at Bien Hoa, their attempts would be widely publicized back in the States. And they knew that over time, if their sheer tenacity and determination – topped off by the mounting numbers of American dead and wounded – reached the home folks, the US would eventually acquire a bad taste for the war. They knew that protest would mount, and that Americans might even bring down their own government.[1]

Since most of the fighting was on the outskirts of the base, I hadn't yet had to "duck and cover." But during the early stages of this firefight with the Charlies I did have to drive in convoy with a fully armed escort; M-60 caliber machine guns front and rear of the bus, plus several other troops manned with M16s. Eventually, the attacks got so severe that we were forced to halt the bus transport of new recruits altogether.

Considering the heavy concentrations of firepower, and the casualties they took – along with our massive air attacks – the NVA and VC fought with a tenacity that struck most American soldiers as unbelievably courageous. In fact, many wounded enemy soldiers continued to fight under conditions under which most of us would have given up. The sight of wounded and bandaged VC or NVA taking the field in combat became commonplace and earned them a soldierly admiration among GIs. Many American troops believed this determination was drug-induced. They certainly seemed rather crazy at times; smiling, grinning, running wild and bouncing off

---

[1] A June 1968 poll found that only 18 percent of Americans believed the country was making progress in Vietnam; a quarter believed America was losing ground, and nearly half felt the U.S. was standing still. Another poll showed only one in ten people still believed allied victory was possible, while two-thirds thought the war would end in compromise. By early 1969, according to the Gallup Poll, an unprecedented majority of Americans had come to believe that the U.S. "made a mistake in sending troops to fight in Vietnam." Weariness with the war was compounded by fears that the fighting would drag on indefinitely. As 1968 ended only a third of the country-35 percent-believed the war would end in the coming year. In short, frustrated and disillusioned, the public was rapidly losing patience with the American mission in Vietnam, and many Americans were looking for a quick end to the war.

trees and other such activity. Some GIs said they could smell marijuana on dead or captured enemy troops. While I can't necessarily verify any of that, it seemed to me that their determined motivation stemmed largely from a clear sense of direction and purpose, instilled and heightened, I'd think, by their Communist Party political cadres. This kind of dedication was a quality that the average American soldier was missing. Our purpose and direction was never really clear.

In spite of the ferocity of their assault, our aggressive air attacks called "bring smoke," shredded them.[2] But even though they took it in the shorts, we lost some troops. A few men were severely wounded and several aircraft were shot up.

We were all sure that after the enemy had sustained such massive retaliation from both ground and air, it would be a cake walk to just go in with the Armed Republic of Vietnam (ARVN) and our own units and mop up. But when ground troops did go in, to their complete surprise they ran directly into dug-in, reinforced and determined units of VC and NVA regulars. Who began banging away fiercely with machine-gun and small arms fire, and an occasional rocket propelled grenade (RPG). This lasted until their survivors melted back into the landscape.

The heavy attacks lasted three to four full days. During the most intense part of the firefight, we were all called out to protect the base's perimeter; most of us just sitting tight, guarding what we called the "berm," with M16s and a few of us with machine guns.

---

2 Many types of aviation were used in this firefight and other areas in Vietnam: Cobra gunships, with their deadly ribbons of mini-gunfire and their 2.75-inch rockets. Another name for the "Cobra Chopper Gunship" was "Spooky" or "Puff the Magic Dragon." The UH-1 was called the "Hewy Chopper." The OH-6A, the light observation chopper, was called the "Loach," the giant CH-47 was named "Chinook Chopper," and the massive load bearing, C-H-54, was the "Sky crane Chopper."

Then things finally settled down and we pretty much got back to our normal duties. The troops at the base got a day off, a well-needed break from the fierce firefight.

Even though I'd been away from most of the major action, I was damn curious about what had gone on. So, without telling my commanding officer, I told several troops in my hooch, including my buddies Frenchie and Wino, to grab their M16s and jump into my bus, and I'd drive them all down to take a look at the aftermath. And several of us (including me) took cameras along. Strictly against Army regulations. We were all sticking our necks out pretty far on this excursion.

When we arrived at one of the major attack sites, I advised the guys on the bus to carry their weapons at all times, stay in groups of no less than three or four, and most importantly, not to wander off too far. After all, this was a risky trek, we were all slightly AWOL, and there was still the possibility we could come face to face with lingering VC or NVA.

The scene was one of complete carnage: a devastated village lying on the outskirts of Bien Hoa city, and very near our army base; dead VC and NVA scattered all over. A gruesome sight. I snapped several pictures and tried to imagine what it must have been like for some of our own guys – like combat photographer Nick Mills, who, we'd heard, had been there with the ARVN. There'd been a couple other photographers shooting the hot, smoky firefight too, and one had been killed. The enemy had counterattacked and Mills and his group were pinned down by machine-gun fire and RPGs. The ARVN had pulled back in a hurry, we heard, dragging their dead and wounded. When Mills made it to safety he found a bunch of guys clustered around a prone figure on the ground. The guy's face was bloody, his uniform was in shreds, and one arm was missing just below the shoulder. A stick of white jagged bone jutted from the bloody stump of the arm. Turned out to be one of the other photographers.

I hadn't been there, but the bitter aftermath hung in the air. The picture before me in that village was one of horror and carnage. There lay a dead Viet Cong, sprawled out on the front steps of a small, burned out and blown apart church. The body was just lying there, a pitiful symbol of this terrible and wasteful war. The stench from the dead and the half burned garbage and debris was enough to make a strong man puke. Many of the bodies were in parts, barely recognizable as having once been human. Others appeared hardly touched but had been wiped out by the intense heat and shock from chopper rocket attacks and the use of devastating napalm.

Here was a scene I would never forget.

We heard that Mills fellow photographer had been in a doorway when the counterattack came. He'd taken a direct hit by an RPG and the doorway had shielded all but his arm from the blast. Somehow, Mills got the photographer to an ARVN ambulance truck, and when the stubborn driver refused to take him (claiming it was only for wounded South Vietnamese), Mills forced the man to take him – with the business end of his M16. The photographer lost his arm, but he lived. The dead VC and NVA sprawled out everywhere in front of me weren't so fortunate. In fact, though I didn't make a body count, I'm sure there were more than 100 scattered throughout the attack site's rubble.

As I walked among the bodies and devastation, a horrible and eerie feeling began to come over me. It was as if the Charlies were watching. After clicking of several pictures, I told one of my comrades, "We'd better start heading back to the bus." He totally agreed, replying, "All this carnage really gives me the creeps."

Some of the area smoldered for several days after the firefight.

If it hadn't been for our air machines – the best weapons we had to use against the Charlies – the ground war, not only in the case of this particular attack but also in the war in general, would have been virtually useless. The grunt in the field relied heavily on air support for nearly everything: ammunition, supplies, hot meals, medevac – and mail from friends and loved ones.

With our overwhelming air power we were sure we could obliterate the enemy. We dropped eight million tons of bombs over North and South Vietnam, quadruple the tonnage during all of World War II. Our estimated aircraft losses were nearly 1000 planes in North Vietnam alone, 3750 overall in North and South Vietnam. Plus an estimated 5000 helicopters. The bombings continued for more than eight years, with 8000 American airmen killed.

My brother Steve (he had served as a security guard at Vung Tau Air Base) and I have a deep respect for those who worked with and manned the vast array of air machines that flew the skies during Vietnam. Having worked in and around two major airfields, we know that had it not been for their mobility and firepower, and the crucial medevac services, there would have been far more casualties than the more than 211,000 dead and wounded America did sustain.

Word certainly got into the American media about this Post-TET attack in 1969. But in my letters, I continued trying to make less of it than it actually was.

February 27, 1969

Dear Mom, Dad, and Marc,

Hi Ho and a bottle of rum. What you all been doing? I think that the worst of my war days might be over. For the past week, old "Charlie" has tried to get us but he has failed. In fact, on the other side of our berm the Viet Cong were slaughtered yesterday by massive air attacks by our planes and choppers and other ground, army-fire. Parts of Bien Hoa town were just torn to bits because Viet Cong had infiltrated the town, so the planes and copters just tore the place apart. I sent slides home to either Steve or Karen of the post-TET offensive attack in Bien Hoa town. The slides, where there are big holes in the buildings and stuff like that. Anyway, things are a little better. Get hold of Karen, she will tell you more of what happened here. Just don't worry, I'm OK! Love Always, Lynn

Speaking of my wife, Karen. . . When I first arrived in Nam she sent me a stream of letters, cards and audiotapes. They'd come in every day or so, and this was wonderfully reassuring. But later the frequency suddenly changed. In fact, it got so damn bad that three and a half months went by and I hadn't received a single letter.

I'd wait in the long mailroom line every day, and come up empty. This left me severely depressed; especially since I'd see my buddies and other troops getting regular mail from loved ones. They'd open their letters and I'd notice their joyful smiles as they read. The only satisfaction I had was to return to the hooch and stare at Karen's beautiful picture on the wall above my bunk. What a lonely and crummy feeling. It all brought back the memory of our last day together in California, at the Oakland Army Center, when she'd seemed preoccupied and wanted to get home in a hurry.

I began (again) to think the unthinkable: that she might be cheating on me. And though I continued to write her at least twice a week, it was a one-way street. She never replied. Then, finally, I got a small package. A reel-to-reel audiotape of our baby daughter, Carrie. With it came a short note, "Here's a tape of your baby girl, hope you enjoy it. Love, Karen."

That was it. Nothing but the note. And even worse, nothing on the tape but the sound of Carrie's crying. I was confused. This didn't make much sense. I played the tape for Wino and Frenchie, and both said that Karen had to be completely nuts to send such a thing.

"It's almost as if she enjoys getting you pissed off," said Frenchie.

Both agreed that to record a few minutes of the crying baby was fine, but not just that alone on the entire tape.

"Maybe she was preoccupied, doing something while the baby was crying," I suggested, trying to be hopeful. Eventually, we all came to the same conclusion: Karen seemed to actually want me to wonder just what she was up to while Carrie was crying. We couldn't figure any other explanation.

"I don't know why she pulls this crap on me," I said to the guys. "As if we haven't got enough to cope with over here. I'm already depressed to the max."

One evening in March of 1969, while I was lying on my bunk swatting mosquitoes, listening to some great sounds on a nearby radio and trying to let go of my depression, the sounds of our friendly fire – rockets blasting off toward the Charlies – which was fairly usual, suddenly changed. Drastically. The rocket sounds were coming in rather than going out! And they were closer than they'd previously been. I'd hear one, then a few seconds later, another. This was weird and creepy. A very unhealthy feeling.

Yep, those eerie sounds were definitely incoming rockets. No time for bullshit. I leaped off the bunk and, just like Specialist Walker had told me, yelled, "Incoming! Incoming!" And then I raced for the sandbagged bunker just outside the hooch. Ten seconds flat to get there. Must have been some kind of record. But not before I stubbed the small toe on my right foot.

In the bunker, shaking like a leaf, I squatted down low into the corner, nursing a severe pain, as the rest of the troops from my hooch tumbled in, some wearing only their skivvies.

We kept our heads and asses down while three or four mortar and rocket rounds smashed into the area immediately near our hooch. One hit only twenty feet away. Another round destroyed a radio communications station – fortunately unmanned at the time. Fortunate too that no one was killed or wounded by this burst of rounds, arriving airmail special delivery, compliments of General Giap. Oh, sure, our feelings were a bit hurt, and we ended up with frayed nerves, and I got a sore toe out of the deal, but that was about it.

After fifteen minutes everything calmed down, we all gradually returned to our bunks and eventually settled into a nervous sleep. But for the next few hours I lay there, one foot off the bunk bed and one eye open, ready to scramble.

And Karen drifted through my mind. What was she up to, I wondered. I'd given up sending her letters, and it would be quite a while before I started again

WHO'S MY ENEMY?

I used to be an Airborne man,
They dropped me from a plane in Vietnam.
Lock and load your M16,
Grab your gear and follow me!
Take the safety off your gun,
Lets go have some combat fun.
Find some enemies, roamin' around,
Take your aim and mow 'em down.
Find some N.V.A. and capture them all,
Line them up against the wall.
Cock your Colt and line up a shot,
Squeeze the trigger and kill the lot.

MILITARY CADENCE (MARCHING REFRAIN)

HIGH JINKS ON THE LBJ RANCH

HIGH JINKS ON THE LBJ RANCH

UNTIL NIXON WAS INAUGURATED IN JANU-
ARY OF 1969, Lyndon Baines Johnson was still running
the war. And even after that I guess a lot of us thought
of Vietnam as doing a stint on the LBJ ranch. Or maybe
in some crazy kind of jungle hotel.[1]

Anyhow. . . One day I got permission from Officer
Gilmore to pick up a 45 caliber semiautomatic pistol,
"just in case."

"You probably won't need the extra weapon," he
said, "But if the Charlies do decide to play more games,
you're gonna need all the firepower you can muster to
protect yourself and your bus load of new recruits."

"Probably won't need the extra weapon?" That's
damn optimistic, I thought, because Charlie, actually
had started acting up again down near the area called
Cong Paddies. Especially after dark. And if he did decide
to take me out, the M16 I already had, plus a chicken-
shit 45 caliber pistol would find me and my busload of
recruits at the ass end of one big, bloody turkey shoot.

Here's something I never quite figured out: the U.S.
Army wanted our butts in the war, but they were willing to put newly arrived replacement recruits on a bus,
transport them through enemy infested areas, even at

---

[1] The Long Binh Jail was nicknamed "The Lyndon Baines Johnson Hotel.

night, and not think a damn thing about issuing them protection against ambush. The militarily intelligent (and logical, I thought) thing to do would have been to at least let me carry an extra stash of weapons and ammo on the bus. It just didn't make any sense. There's an old saying that applies here: "There's a right way, a wrong way – and the Army way."

Anyhow, I went to the arms room to get the 45 and a box of rounds, as well as more ammo for my M16. I also wanted the arms room specialist to check out the M16 to make absolutely sure that it was in tiptop shape.

"Bowman, do you go to Long Binh base almost every day?" Specialist Jackman asked me.

"Sure do. Five, sometimes six days a week. Why do you ask?"

"Have you ever been over by or at the shipping depot in Long Binh?" he went on, in a somewhat confidential manner.

"Yeah, I've been there a few times. I know exactly where it is, if that's what you're getting at."

"Well, here's the deal, Bowman. Can you keep your mouth shut?"

"I guess so," I replied, "But what the hell are you working on, Jackman?"

He looked around to make sure no one was watching, then leaned in close and, practically whispering, said, "I need to put one over on my chicken-shit commanding officer, the son-of-a-bitch. He made me go over and clean out the latrine for two solid weeks, cleaning urinals, shitty toilets, walls and floors, because I left a damned M16 rifle out on the counter overnight. It happened like this, see; my work duty was practically over and suddenly shells started comin' in from the friggin Charlies. So I had to split for the closest sand bunker.

Then, after it all calmed down, I went straight to my hooch for the evening."

"So, did you just forget about the rifle on the counter or what?" I asked.

"No, I knew the damned rifle was there, but I didn't think it was a big deal. After all there's hundreds of rifles everywhere in the arms room. That lifer SOB, the prick, thinks we're on some kind of ridiculous stateside duty over here in this hellhole. If he pulled that kind of crap in some boonie infantry camp, or out humping with some ground pounders, someone would rifle the bastard in the back of the head or frag the motha' when he least expected it. Blow his ass to smithereens. That's what the sucker deserves."

I nodded in agreement.

"So here's the deal, Bowman, I'm gonna get some high class, heavy duty revenge on that peckerhead. I'm gonna ship some weapons home."

"You mean to the States?"

"That's exactly what I plan to do, send em' smack dab to my home in Texas. But you see, I've got a real problem. I can get my hands on all kinds of stuff, but I can't get it off the base. That's where you come in, Bowman, because you get out of this Godforsaken place with your bus practically every day."

"What do you want me to do? What's my part in this? Look, you tell me the plan and then I'll decide if I wanna get involved. Anyway, Jackman, what's in the deal for me if I go along with this crazy idea?"

"How's about a brand new, never been out of the box, never been fired, M16?"

I said, "That's fine. But could you also throw in a 45-caliber pistol?" That sounded damn good, to find a brand new M16 and a 45 waiting for me when I got home.

"No problem," said Jackman, "But you need to check out our shippin' source at the depot in Long Binh, first."

I was still turning all this over in my head. "Yeah," I said, "But do you realize what can happen if just one of these troops I talk to at the shippin' depot decides to blow the whistle?"

"You take care of your end, and I'll take care of mine," he replied. "No sweat."

That sort of clinched it.

"By the way Jackman, don't forget to check out my M16," I said, remembering what I come in for in the first place, "I'll be back in a couple of hours. OK?"

"No problem, Bowman, I'll have it all sittin' right here on the counter."

When I returned for my ammo and my two weapons, I told Jackman I'd see him in a day or so to let him know what had come up with my contact at the depot.

"And, Jackman, you'd better cross your damned fingers," I added, "Because if this goes haywire we'll both be up shit-creek without a paddle."

"No sweat," he said again, real cool.

Back at "in processing" to take my daily trip of new replacement recruits over to their units in Long Binh, I kept wondering what the hell I was about to get into. I dropped off the recruits then headed out again. I didn't have a lot of time to screw off because I had to get back over to the 90th Replacement for the next shipment of new recruits.

Once, at the shipping depot, I walked into a large storage area and started looking around, searching for a likely troop that might want to join in our crusade to dispatch some weapons back to the world. This was going to be a risky business. If I chose the wrong dude the whole scheme could end up in disaster. Still, I knew that if I was going to do this I had to step in and get my feet wet.

Nearby, a PFC was stacking footlockers and moving duffle bags around. This troop seemed to be a likely candidate, so I went over, said hello, and started to feel the situation out.

"I've got a small problem," I said. "I'd like to ship out about a thousand rounds of Charlie-captured 7.62 ammo back home to California. Stuff I got from an infantry troop over at the 199th Light Infantry Brigade. It was captured after a firefight with some VC north of here."

He seemed interested.

"I've also got several AK47's and SKS Soviet and Chinese communist rifles that were captured," I added.

Guess I sounded pretty convincing because he replied, "What's the problem, Bowman?" (he'd picked up my name from my fatigues), "I can ship practically anything out of here. And I mean just about anything."

Unless he was all bullshit, it looked like I'd lucked out first go. Although he seemed busier than the famous one-armed paperhanger, here he was sitting on a footlocker, shooting the shit with me. So I decided to cut to the chase before some snoopy lifer officer or non-com happened to come by and boot my ass out of there.

"You really can ship almost anything, Johnson?" I asked. (I'd clocked his name from his fatigues like he had mine.)

"Bowman, just give me a try. I told you, I can ship anything." Then he looked at me hard and said, "But if it's hot stuff there'll be a price."

"Can you ship me out two or three M16s and a couple of 45 caliber pistols?"

"So that's what you want me to do, ship out some weapons and the thousand rounds of Viet Cong ammo?" The way Johnson asked the question made me a bit nervous. But now that I'd jumped into the water I had to keep swimming. Keep cool, I told myself; everything will probably work out fine. "Just forget the 7.62 ammo for now," I said, deciding to ditch the bullshit story, "We'll worry about that later."

"No real problem, whatever you want to ship is okay. Like I said, Bowman, I can do it, but you gotta get me one of those M16 Charlie-killers."

Then he told me the drill.

"Bowman, now you listen to me, this is serious business. I want you to wrap everything in rubber, something like inner tube material."

"What the hell's that for?"

"Listen up! Believe me, this is the way to go. Just get a hold of some inner tubes at any motor pool, new or used, it doesn't matter. Cut the rubber down into workable layers and then break the M16s down and completely wrap all the parts and the pistols with it, not allowing anything to show. No exposed metal or parts at all, understand? Then be absolutely sure to secure the rubber wrapping so that no gun part can fall out or come undone."

Just then, a staff sergeant walked into the area. "Oh, shit," Johnson said under his breath, "I've got to get back to work, my hard-ass boss is looking over here.

Check back with me tomorrow or the next day, Bowman, about the same time."

"Okay see you later," I said and hurried off back to my bus.

Two days later, after checking in with Specialist Jackman back in the arms room, I returned to the shipping depot and told Johnson it was a go for the shipment. I also assured him that I'd bring him an M16 rifle as payment, probably the next week.

The next week came and went. For days, I'd been stewing, thinking about this crap of wrapping all of the broken down M16 parts and 45 caliber pistols with inner tube material. PFC Johnson's voice and body language had been so damn serious when he instructed me how to wrap everything that there didn't seem to be any room for error. I had also heard through the grapevine that if a soldier got caught taking U.S. Government property, he might as well kiss his sorry ass goodbye.

But I was conflicted. I could almost taste the brand new M16 and 45 that would await my arrival back home. Still, if the weapons Johnson would ship out had to be prepared in such a seriously foolproof manner, maybe it was too damn risky. Back and forth I went in my head. Finally, I concluded that I wanted nothing to do with sending those weapons back to the world. I completely chickened out on the deal and never returned to the shipping depot. (At least not in regard to shipping out hot government property.) Couldn't quite push myself over the hump.

But now I had a real dilemma: how was I going to smooth over this sticky situation? What the hell would I tell Specialist Jackman down at the arms room? He was 100% committed, and practically salivating to ship the weapons out. For a while, procrastination set in. I let Jackman think everything was still a go. While all the time I was trying to come up with a good excuse for changing my mind. Finally, a bullshit idea occurred to me. I'd tell him that the shipping dude, PFC Johnson, had been transferred to another unit, so our little plan was squashed.

But then I realized that Jackman wouldn't fall for some half-baked story like that, so I scratched the idea. Finally, I kicked myself in the ass and went down to the arms room to get it over with. "It's all over but the shoutin'," I confessed. "I've got no damned balls to carry out our little plan."

Jackman starred icicles into me. A look of total disgust.

"I'll tell you what I can do," I said, trying to appease him, "Get me a piece of paper and I'll write down Johnson's landline number at the depot. Then maybe you can contact him and strike a deal direct. He seems to be very receptive. And do mention my name because for a while there we had one heck of a working relationship going."

"I suppose that's worth a try," said Jackman, still looking pissed off.

"I'm real sorry about pulling out," I apologized, "but I'm sure you can put something together with Johnson." I left the arms room feeling a bit foolish, but mighty relieved. If anybody could carry out a plan, Jackman surely could. I had to take my hat off to him for having the balls to continue. On the other hand, I was still a bit disappointed with my chickenshit lack of courage.

After sleeping on this over night, I decided to go see Jackman one more time with some friendly advice. "By the way Jackman," I began, trying to lighten things up, "Don't do anything stupid, like leaving any more items out on your work counter, so those bastard lifers can kick your ass and send you back down for more latrine duty."

Jackman chuckled. But I think he was just trying to show his decent side. Deep down, I suspect he was thoroughly disgusted with me.

"Most important of all," I continued, sounding more serious, "When you contact Johnson over at the Long Binh shipping depot, be careful. Some big ears could definitely put a serious dent in you if they crash your little party. By the way," I added, as a kind of face-saving parting shot, "If you have any trouble working out your little weapons deal with Johnson, get a hold of me. I may change my mind and jump right back into this thing."

"Thanks for the good advice Bowman," Jackman said, sounding real friendly again, "I'll keep that in mind and let you know if I need you!"

I left the weapons room feeling much relieved. A tiny bit guilty still, but damn glad there was no chance I might someday have to face a court-martial or who knows, maybe a stint in the Lyndon Baines Johnson Hotel.

And yeah, it did gall me a little to realize that there'd be no brand new U.S. Army issue weapons waiting for me when I got back to California.

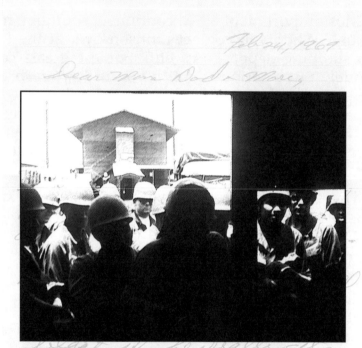

I'D WAIT IN THE LONG MAILROOM LINE EVERY DAY, AND COME UP EMPTY

ON THE EDGE

ON THE EDGE

Black are the brooding clouds and troubled the deep waters when the sea of thought, first heaving from a calm, gives up its dead.

CHARLES DICKENS

Nothing is more capable of troubling our reason, and consuming our health, than secret notions of jealousy in solitude.

APHRA BEHN, ENGLISH WRITER (1640-1689)

There is only one universal passion: fear.

GEORGE BERNARD SHAW

EACH DAY WHEN THE MAIL WAS AVAILABLE, we would wait patiently to collect it. Any kind of mail from the free world was extremely important and gratifying to the troops in Nam. Day after day, I'd wait hopefully in the long line. Maybe this day, I thought, would be my lucky one. Maybe there'd be a letter from Karen. But no damned way. All my waiting was in vain, a complete waste of time. There was nothing at all from her, not even a small card to say she still cared. Nothing.

Occasionally, I'd get something from my good brother, Steve who had served his Vietnam tour in 1966 and 1967. He seemed very concerned about me, and at least he wrote, unlike my disrespectful wife. I also received letters and cards weekly from my parents, usually from my mother. Most fathers are too macho to write or are preoccupied. Even though my father didn't write, I knew he cared and was concerned about me. I could sense it through what my mother had to say in her cards and letters.

As more time passed, I noticed that my brother and parents wrote less and less about my wife, Karen. They sensed that it really bothered me that she wasn't writing. That it was having a devastating effect on my state of mind. In previous letters I had asked if they knew what she was up to. I also told them I couldn't understand why she wasn't writing to me anymore. I certainly had my suspicions, but just didn't want to accept the possibility that she was whoring around. Finally, my family stopped mentioning my wife entirely in their letters. Of course, this convinced me that they knew most everything that was going on. I convinced myself that they probably even knew who she was screwing around with, but it became obvious that neither my brother nor my parents wanted to pass on unpleasant news.

Gradually, I began to rebel. I sent less and less mail to the wife I was sure was being unfaithful. Eventually, I stopped writing altogether. Grief set in, and I became even more depressed than when I'd talked the situation over with Wino and Frenchie. The whole thing became so bad that even thinking about it made me physically sick. Eventually, since Karen's lack of writing was having such a devastating effect on me, I didn't even want to get in the mail line. But since the rest of my family was still writing, I managed to get to mail call about once a week. The best thing, I figured, was to just try not to dwell on it.

There's that old saying, "misery loves company." And by this point I was damn miserable.

One day, a comrade began to strike up a friendship with me. Specialist Becker was his name, and he worked as one of the many office clerks within our administrative and logistics complexes. Becker didn't seem to be a very outgoing sort of guy, or one of the normal types within our unit. He was overweight and really didn't fit in or give me the impression that he was any kind of a lady's man, that's for sure. But he seemed friendly enough, and I needed friends.

After we became better acquainted, he told me that many of the troops he worked with made fun of him and really didn't want much to do with him. In the beginning, I sort of felt sorry for the guy, so I didn't mind him coming over to my hooch once in a while for a visit. Clearly, he was a very well read person and seemed extremely intelligent. He always wore horned rimmed glasses, like the kids in school we used to call "teacher's pet" or "four eyes." The nerd type, the kind that always had his nose stuffed in some damn book and managed to breeze through high school and college with a straight A in every class.

One evening, Becker told me that while he was down at the camp club having a soda, one of the troops that he worked with called him a "nerdy, faggot, queer bait, son-of-a-bitch." He had also told Becker if he didn't stop looking at him and his friends, he was going to come over and bust him in the chops.

Though I didn't think much about Becker's story, in time I began to wonder.

For a while, in the beginning of our short friendship, I kind of thought he was just lonely and wanted a friend. And indeed, with all that was going on around us, you really did need friends in Nam. Especially a guy like me, and considering everything I was sure was going on with Karen.

Becker would usually come over to my hooch in the evenings, when we were all done with our daily duties.

We'd sat around and shot the shit and, as the current 60s hits played over our military radio station, AFVN, talk about how eager we were to get out of Nam. This one evening, a very warm one, Specialist Becker came by. It was rather late, later than his usual visits; I was worn out from a bunch of extra driving, and about ready to fall asleep. We chatted for a few minutes then he began telling me about an experience he'd just had.

"When I was down at the latrine just now," he began, "A troop taking a piss in the urinal asked me to suck him off. Can you believe that, Bowman?"

I said, "Are you sure that's what he said? Maybe you didn't hear him correctly?"

"I'm absolutely sure."

"That's kind of disgusting, don't you think?"

"Well, that all depends," said Becker.

But now, I thought something strange was going on, so it seemed like a good time to change the subject. "Hey, Becker," I said, "Listen to that great tune on the radio!"

Becker continued rambling on, but his one-sided conversation was beginning to bore me to death, and I really wanted him to get the hell out of there. Maybe, I thought, if I pretend to fall asleep, he'll catch on and split. So I lay back on my bunk and made like I was drifting off. But he continued flapping his jaws.

Then, to my disgusted surprise, Becker suddenly put his hand midway between the ankle and knee of my left leg. I continued to fake like I'd fallen asleep – while thinking to myself that maybe it was time to jump up and kick this four-eyed faggot's ass. Because now, I was sure that's what he was.

In some mysterious and almost miraculous way, like

he'd read my mind, Becker seemed to get the message. A moment later he just got up from the edge of my bunk and abruptly walked out of the hooch. Needless to say, this was a huge relief.

What a lonely, depressing feeling. Here I am, I thought, halfway around the world and stuck in a damn useless war heading nowhere, and I get propositioned! At the time, of course, I didn't give spit about the idea that gays could probably get lonely too. The only thing on my mind was what my phony bitch of a wife was probably doing back in California, while here in Nam some perverted, overweight fag was trying to put the make on me.

This only added to the misery of dwelling on Karen. As much as possible, I tried not to think about her. Fortunately, there were other occasional distractions.

In the shaving kit I'd brought along from California was a small green bottle of Brut after-shave lotion. I didn't much care for the fragrance, but on occasion I'd splash some on my face anyhow. It sort of brought back the more pleasant memories of home.

On one particular day with slack time between bus deliveries, I was catching up on writing to my brother and parents, when a Vietnamese friend, Miss Lee – who was one of the hooch maids – came by to say hello. ("Miss Lee" wasn't her actual Vietnamese name, but that's what it sounded like to me, so that's what I called her. And she *was* just a friend. No hanky-panky in the back of the bus.)

HOOCH MAIDS

She sidled up to me in a flirting sort of way – which wasn't usual for her – put her hand on my face, and then smelled her hand. She seemed fascinated with the after-shave lotion smell she'd detected.

"*Law-de' homa ki monoy,*" I said, which means, "Give me a kiss, honey!" Then, I laughed and hugged her in a friendly way and said, "This smell is Brut after shave lotion."

"Boot," she repeated.

"No, Lee. . . you say, '*Brut,*' not 'boot!' "

Over time, Miss Lee began to pronounce the name "Brut" correctly and began getting real funny and more talkative towards me, and started calling me "Mista Brut."

Eventually, I gave her the rest of my bottle of Brut. She seemed extremely grateful, and maintained a solid fascination for the strong fragrance.

Periodically, I'd run into Lee at the base. One day when she came by to say hello I noticed the "Brut" fragrance lingering around her. She began making somewhat crazy gestures and pointing and pulling at her hair. In some odd way she managed to convey to me that she'd put some of the stuff in her hair! "Makes bugs go away," she said, and laughed.

Mosquitoes were a huge, pesky problem in our area, especially during the rainy (monsoon) season. So pesky, in fact, that we joked that they could almost carry a soldier off. The troops called them "mini-choppers." Apparently, Lee had put some of the shaving lotion in her hair to ward them off.

Now I know why I was never really fond of the Brut after-shave lotion smell. It's so damned repulsive, so pungent and potent, that it actually works like a great insect repellant!

The business with Lee and the Brut had been a light, amusing interlude in my stress over Karen. The next incident, however, wouldn't be so light. In a way, I became a real brute.

Among my bus driving duties, down in the civilian city of Bien Hoa I continued to pick up the hooch maids that worked at our base. Over time the bus became more and more crowded, and the hooch maids would yell and fight over the seats. Gradually, a rebel group of hooch maids, not my regular bunch, began to climb aboard. They had either missed their own rides, or were lazy opportunists that waited for any kind of a pickup. For a while, I didn't give a damn. But eventually these extra "bastard rebel gooks" as I thought of them (that was the lingo; at the time, most Vietnamese were "gooks" to most of us), created a major congested overload, because they'd become blatantly persistent and wouldn't budge an inch. Nor could they easily be discouraged, even when I tried to aggressively shut the bus door to cut off the rude inflow.

One particular mamasan began to yell at me on a regular basis. She pulled this shit every day as she got on the bus, along with her tag-along rebel group. She'd even double up her fist on occasion and stick it in my face as she cursed and screamed out something vile in Vietnamese. In the beginning, I wasn't too bothered by this nonsense. After all, in my book she was just some "pint sized, gook bitch." But in time it progressed into a nerve-wracking nightmare.

One morning in the city of Bien Hoa, as I loaded up at my usual stop, my regular hooch maids began to get really pissed off. The pushing, fighting and screaming between my regulars and the rebels began to escalate to enormous proportions. It got so damn bad that I could hardly see out of my side mirrors or see out the right front window of the bus. I couldn't hear myself think.

Finally, the crowding became so great that I couldn't even shut the door. The women were stuffed everywhere, packed like sardines in the aisle, and even standing on the stairway with the door jammed wide open. To shift gears without pushing one of them out of the way had become nearly impossible. I firmly believed that given the chance they would have started climbing on top of the bus in order to catch a ride.

I decided that I wasn't going to take this crap any longer. I turned to my Vietnamese friend, Miss Lee, who was on the bus and asked her to tell the leader of the rebels that she and her group were to get off the bus. "Like right now, and never try to get on again!"

The rebel mamasan was standing on the bus stairway at the time, and as soon as Lee started to translate, the rebel started screaming at me. Though I had no idea what she was saying, her manner told me that it was fairly vile. Miss Lee turned to me and said, "She not getting off bus." And, Miss Lee added, she'd said something to the effect that if I continued to bother them she was going to get her Viet Cong friends and relatives to take care of me.

Up until now, I'd been simmering. This brought everything to a boil. A combination of fear and madness shot through me like a bolt of lightning. Still, I controlled myself long enough to make one more last ditch effort. "Tell her," I said to Miss Lee, "That if she and her group don't get off the bus pronto, I'll blow her damned head off!" [1] Then I reached over and grabbed my M16 off the dashboard and pointed the business end directly into the rebel's face.

In a harsh tone, my friend again told her to get off the bus. I waited, with my heart in my throat, for a

[1] In my fury, I'm sure Miss Lee didn't quite understand all my words, but she certainly got the intent.

response. What I got back was a nasty, scowling stare. Miss Lee, clearly nervous, indicated that this woman sometimes carried a knife. Then my friend tried to talk with the rebel again. I waited, maintaining an eagle eye on this disgruntled woman, and wondered where this conversation was going to lead. After they'd exchanged a few more hot words Miss Lee turned to me again and, looking extremely worried, said, "She say she will gut you out like dog." Meaning she intended to slice me open and disembowel me. Then the gook bitch reached into a canvas satchel strapped over her shoulder, pulled out a sharp-looking knife and pointed it directly at me.

That did it. I blew my top. I immediately jacked a round into my M16, jumped out of my seat and pointed the barrel at her head. "Get off this damned bus!" I yelled.

She stood her ground, pointing the blade and trying to back me down. Out of sheer terror, I almost pulled the trigger. I actually started to squeeze. I was ready to blow her away. Fortunately, I stopped just in time, because she was standing in front of a couple other women on the stairway, and I likely would have taken out three of them with one shot. Instead, I kicked her hand that was holding the knife. It dislodged, hit the top of the bus with a clang and fell on the steps behind her. In the next instant I charged down the steps, pushing the rebel out past the others and knocking her to the ground outside.

By now, I was in a total rage. Her threats about sicking the Viet Cong on me had whacked my brain. That was the crusher. I grabbed her by one arm and jerked her up off the ground, practically dragging her to the side of the bus. She stood there, still determined and screaming at me nonstop in unbelievable anger. She had a lot of guts for such a small woman. She tried to hit me with closed fists, and even spit on me.

Then she made a sudden, aggressive move in the direction of the open bus door. Instantly, I flashed on the knife that I'd stepped over when I pushed her off the bus. At this moment, all I could think about was the threat to my life. I had to stop her from getting that knife – like now!

I came completely unglued. Up came the butt of my M16, into the side of her head. Down she went. Then I stomped her in the head and neck several times, just as I would any enemy. I actually wanted to put her away. I wanted to kill her. As she lay there twitching and jerking like a chicken with its head cut off I paused for a split second, flashing back on a childhood memory of a day back home in Northern California when my father chopped off a chicken's head with a hatchet and it continued to flip and flop all around the yard.

I got back on the bus in a state of shock. For several moments, my head was in a tailspin. Then it dawned on me: where was the gook's weapon? I frantically started to search for the knife; on the ground outside the bus steps, on the steps, and all around my bus seat. I panicked and screamed at the silent and staring hooch maids, "Where the hell is that damned knife!?"

Miss Lee started to say something, and at about the same time one of my other regular hooch maids, timid and scared, handed the knife over to me.

Apparently, when I was outside taking care of business with the Viet Cong-threatening rebel, this gracious little hooch maid took it upon herself to pick up the knife. For a split second, I wondered what she intended doing with it, but I soon concluded that she was acting in a friendly, responsible manner by keeping it away from any other deranged rebel that might have had evil intentions.

I took a good look at the knife. It was actually a common butter knife of the sort generally found in a silverware drawer. More than likely, I concluded, it had been taken from our mess hall at the base. Though butter knives are not sharp, on closer inspection I realized that someone had crudely honed this one to near razor sharpness, making it a seriously dangerous weapon. This rebel Vietnamese, I'm sure, was sympathetic to the Viet Cong.

Though I'd come within an eyelash of shooting her stone dead, I hadn't wanted to draw a crowd or expose myself with the loud sound of gunfire. I was right in the middle of civilian Bien Hoa, after all, and surrounded by thousands and thousands of peasants and villagers. God only knows how many might have been undercover VC. My major concern was that I was completely cut off from any armed support, and the situation could easily have become seriously ugly.

The rebel and her crew never rode my bus again. I never found out for sure, but I suspect that she died from the injuries she received from my rifle butt and my frenzied boot stomping. Something I couldn't quite figure out, however, was that each time I tried to talk to my friend Miss Lee about this horrible incident, she'd become very nervous and evade my questions.

From then on, whenever I drove my bus through the city of Bien Hoa, I was running scared.

After this, the hurt and disappointment over my feelings about my wife Karen was reduced somewhat. I guess the incident on the bus had gotten rid of a lot of tension. Or maybe it was just that I'd become more preoccupied with self-preservation than fretting over an unfaithful wife. Still, for quite a time I made some dangerous decisions and did many crazy whacked out things, like going AWOL without a weapon in places where I might have been in harm's way. Or not bothering to check to see if engine repairs had been made on the bus, which could have put me and a load of troops in a precarious position if it had broken down during an enemy attack.

With a mixture of grief, depression, loneliness and anger running through me, I slowly began to realize that if I didn't get myself back together the Charlies would eventually have their way. The war was bad enough; I didn't need to make it worse by being stupid and careless. I had to somehow control my depression. Or at least minimize it.

Gradually, I found that if I put my wife in the same category as the VC and the NVA, I could alter the state of my mind. She'd become the enemy. I mentally began to put up an imaginary wall between us. A shell of protection. A barrier that I wouldn't allow her to penetrate. At first it seemed like a crazy idea, and maybe it wasn't the best way to go about this, but it gradually began to work. I slowly started to regain my self-esteem and composure. I even started thinking of the pleasant things in life, like a "rest and recreation" (R and R) to Sydney, Australia. Australia would be a better place, since I wasn't about to take my R and R in Hawaii, like the other married soldiers. Not with a wife who I was convinced was being unfaithful.

For several months I'd been heading down a long, dark tunnel. Now I could begin to see some light at the end. I simply wasn't going to let my suspicions about Karen destroy my self-esteem; I wouldn't let her continue to break me down mentally. Between the business on the bus and my other screw-ups, I had come so close to death that I could almost smell it. On a few occasions, death was very near because of the war alone, but other times I took too damned many risky chances, placing myself in harm's way due to my grief and loneliness.

So for now, the imaginary wall between my wife and me was working. But I wasn't confident it would last. And the conflicts were still there, inside. Buried for a while, but still there. I truly loved Karen. I cherished her, but I couldn't deal with what I was sure was going on back home.

Meanwhile, the war, both in Vietnam and within myself, dragged on.

WHO'S MY ENEMY?

You can hardly make a friend in a year,
but you can easily offend one in an hour.

CHINESE PROVERB

HOME FOLKS

*Hanging onto resentment is letting someone
you despise live rent-free in your head.*

Ann Landers

Jealousy is all the fun you think they had.

Erica Jong

IN LONG BINH with the bus one day to pick up new
recruits, one of my fellow bus drivers announced over
the microphone a name I instantly recognized: Buck
Sergeant Webster, the guy from Fort Hood, Texas whose
wife Karen had mistakenly called the police on about
her missing watch. Until that point, we'd all been great
friends, and I desperately wanted to apologize for my
wife's false accusation that his wife, Ann, had stolen her
damn heirloom.

After I'd gathered up my new recruits and checked
their records, I announced Webster's name over the
mic, then waited a couple minutes. No response. Since
I really wasn't sure if he was actually out there among
the large group of replacement troops, or even if this
was the same man I was looking for, I gave it another
try: "Sergeant David Webster; Sergeant David Webster,
please report to window number three."

Within a minute or so, and somewhat to my surprise,
the buck sergeant appeared. I recognized him immediately; it was indeed Sergeant Webster from Fort Hood.

I greeted him at the window, saying, "Hello, Sarge. Do you remember me?"

He looked at me then immediately did a quick about-face. I had no chance to apologize about my wife; he just split. I had desperately wanted to make amends, to let this dude know that it was Karen's fault, not mine. And since he was the first troop I'd actually recognized since arriving in Nam, I saw this as a reason to chat. I wanted to at least wish him good luck.

Later on, just before I started to load the next batch of new recruits, I made one more last ditch effort. After searching through gobs of recruits I finally located him, sitting on a bench with several others, waiting to leave for his duty assignment on his designated bus.

"Hello, sergeant," I said, smiling, "I just wanted to let you know how sorry I am about –"

"Get the hell out of here, asshole," he replied, cutting me off. "Leave me the hell alone."

Well, at that point I didn't have much of a choice. I turned around and left. Can't say I didn't try. Actually, after what my wife's accusation had dragged Webster and his wife through, I couldn't blame him for still holding one hell of heavy-duty grudge. If I were in his shoes I'd probably have been pissed off too.

The next contact from home was a bit more pleasant. Well, in some ways.

In mid-April of 1969, Karen finally sent me a short note. Maybe half a dozen lines. In it, she told me that a young Air Force troop wanted to visit me. I was supposed to contact him a few days later, as soon as he arrived at the Bien Hoa Air Base. Once we'd made contact, said my wife, he would snag a ride to Bien Hoa

Army Base, where we could meet after work hours, at my convenience.

And just like she said, when he came in I got in touch and we met at my base. Good to hook up with someone from close to home, I thought, even though I didn't know him. We jawed a while, then hoofed it on down to the base club, where we swapped stories over a few beers. He told me that his parents were good friends of my wife and her parents back in Northern California. How close, I didn't know. Until much later, when I discovered that my damned wife had *such* a close friend of this Air Force troop's brother that they'd become part-time lovers.

But for now, ignorance was bliss.

Several damn cute Vietnamese gals were entertaining in a band at the club that evening. The troop commented about how good looking some of them were, especially the half French ones.

"If you think they're good looking this early in the game," I laughed, "Just wait until you've been in Nam a little longer. A few more beers and a few more months under your belt, and they'll become Bridget Bardot."

Too darn many beers. But I didn't care whether they looked like Bridget Bardot or not; I had to go to the john. While I was at the urinal, a huge black troop came barging in. He started yelling at a much smaller white troop standing there next to me. The white troop started backing up, and said he was sorry about something and tried desperately to get away from the clearly pissed-off black dude.

Then, with a right hand haymaker, the black troop smashed the white troop square in the mouth, smashing his upper lip into his teeth and bloodying him up pretty good before he turned and stomped out. Good thing he left, because he probably could've killed that little white troop.

For a split second the extreme difference in their sizes pissed me off. It seemed unfair and very lopsided; like a heavyweight taking on a featherweight. But since I didn't have a clue what was going on or what had happened before the black troop came into the latrine, I kept my nose out of it. While I'm a big guy, if I had tried the big black troop on for size, I might've had one hell of a tiger by the tail. There always seemed to be some tension between the black and white troops in Vietnam. They'd get into arguments, spats, and sometimes fights. Racially, it was far from a perfect situation.

I helped clean the white troop's face and mouth with a wet paper towel. Then, still wondering what the fight was about (if you'd call it a fight), went back out to my table to join my Air Force companion.

The Air Force troop and I had a few more beers, bullshitted for a while longer then said goodbye and retired for the evening. He hitched a ride to Bien Hoa Air Base, and I walked back to the hooch and crashed in my bunk. I fell asleep fast, that fight in the john still on my mind. And if I had known then what I later discovered about the Air Force troop's brother balling my wife, I'm not sure what I would have done. Even though this guy was only the brother.

TALENTED VIETNAMESE BAND PLAYING AT BASE CLUB

LYNN AND AIR FORCE TROOP

FRENCHIE TOOK THIS PICTURE OF ME WHILE WE WERE AWOL IN SAIGON

MAIN DRAG IN DOWNTOWN SAIGON

AWOL TO SAIGON

Saigon was an addicted city, and we were the drug: the corruption of children, the mutilation of young men, the prostitution of women, the humiliation of the old, the division of the family, the division of the country – it had all been done in our name. . . . The French city . . . had represented the opium stage of the addiction. With the Americans had begun the heroin phase.

JAMES FENTON, POET

FRENCHIE AND I GOT ALL BEERED UP down at the base club one early afternoon on our day off.

"Hey, Bowman," he said, "Let's go get us a piece of ass down in Saigon."

The crazy bugger! He acted as if Saigon was just around the corner. We talked it over and headed out anyway, hitching a lift on a deuce and a half and trucked our way down Highway 1.

AWOL was some serious shit, but we really didn't give a damn as long as we didn't get caught by the MPs or run into some Charlies. Neither of us had a weapon, which didn't set to well with me, but Frenchie didn't seem to care. He had not a worry in the world because he was stupid as a rock. On the other hand, I knew better. What the hell was my excuse?

We hit Saigon with a bang, and right away decided that we wanted to ride in one of the famous old-fashioned Vietnamese cyclo carts; sort of like rickshaws, powered by a papasan pedaling a bike.

By the time we got to the big city, Frenchie and I were starving, so shortly after a pleasant cyclo cart ride we located a nice Vietnamese restaurant, a swanky place I might say, with bright white tablecloths, rolled up napkins, ceiling fans and fancy-dressed waiters. The works. Somehow we broke through the language barrier, using all kinds of back and forth tidbits of verbiage and hand signals with the congenial and patient waiter, and finally enjoyed a fairly decent Vietnamese meal and hot tea.

Then we went in search of some good-looking gals at one of the many "boom boom" parlors – your normal Vietnamese whorehouse – generally connected with many of the drinking establishments. Without any idea where the heck to go, we started asking around. Two GIs with a serious language barrier searching for ass in Saigon; what a pair. For a while, we had one heck of a time. Then we ran into an elderly Vietnamese man, a papasan who fortunately for us could understand a little English. We made a half-ass verbal arrangement with him. In exchange for info on some good-looking gals, we'd purchase some items he wanted at a military PX in the city.

Even though (because of the language barrier) I wasn't totally sure of this deal, we took a chance and purchased the goods for the papasan. Then he started to lead us down a scuzzy back alley toward where, he said, we'd find some hookers. "This place looks like the shits," I whispered to Frenchie. "It even smells like the shits, and it gives me some serious jitters." Still, Frenchie acted like he didn't have a fear in the world. The guy had plenty of guts, that's for damn sure.

The elderly Vietnamese guided us through dark alleys laced with small dwellings. Dozens of burn barrels gave off the putrid stench of smoldering shit. The odor was strong enough to burn the hairs right out of your nostrils and scald your eyeballs at the same time. What a sex-crazed GI won't do for a pleasurable piece of ass, I thought to myself.

For a while, I suspected this papasan was leading us on a wild goose chase. Or maybe the unthinkable, right into a Charlie trap. Plus which, it was most important that we not get caught in Saigon by some nasty-ass MPs, so we had to keep our eyes peeled.

By the time we finally arrived at the boom boom parlor, I was in a nervous sweat. Not so, Frenchie; he was calm as a clam. He had only one thing on his mind: women! Don't get me wrong, I thoroughly enjoy the hedonistic pleasures, but not at the expense of having my butt blown off.

Finally, we arrived at a shack where several Vietnamese whores stood around outside. The elderly papasan said something to them. Introducing us, probably. Though in his Vietnamese lingo, he could as easily have been telling them to cut off our friggin' dicks. We wouldn't have known the difference.

We chose our women and got with the program. Some of these Vietnamese gals weren't half bad looking. One or two seemed like they were French-Vietnamese.

So Frenchie and I got taken into separate rooms. The gal I was with really wasn't into the sex as much as I was, and before long, her hand and facial gestures indicated that she'd had enough. But I hadn't. I wanted my fair share, my ecstasy. Although this crummy, rundown place gave me a bad feeling, my physical desires had taken over. And I did succeed.

After we finished our business at the boom boom parlor we headed back down several smoke-filled alleys to a wider, better-looking street. Then, just when we thought we had it made in the shade, the ax fell. A hard-core MP spotted us. Damn it to hell! A pencil-necked, skinny-ass fellow, he hailed us to come across the congested street. He just stood there looking pissed off, with the typical cop stare attitude, his hands planted firmly on his hips.

"Let me see your passes or orders from your military unit that say you can be here in Saigon," he barked.

Frenchie started searching through his jungle fatigues, as if he was trying to locate the damned papers. I figured we were screwed. Then Frenchie said to me, "Bowman, do you have those orders from our commander?"

I quickly picked up on his ploy and started doing the same as Frenchie, rambling through my pockets.

Frenchie, putting on a good show, went on with, "Bowman, I think we lost the son-of-a-bitchin' orders. They must have blown out of our fatigues on the way down Highway 1. Maybe they blew out in the back of that deuce and a half."

Oh, this is real great, I'm thinking! Now what the hell are we going to do?

"I guess you boys are AWOL then," said the MP, sneering.

I started laughing a bit, and Frenchie soon joined in. We couldn't help ourselves. This character was obviously in pig heaven; proud as hell to be a typical, decked out MP. To top it off, the troop was so scrawny, maybe five-foot six and 125 pounds soaking wet, and with such an unbelievably high-pitched voice, that he cracked Frenchie and me up. To add to this bizarre scene, he had to constantly pull up his heavy, gun-toting trousers to keep the lower end of his nightstick from scraping the ground. We could see that the black paint at the lower end had already been worn off. He reminded me of Barney Fife, the heavy-handed, skinny, pencil-necked deputy sheriff of Mayberry on the Andy Griffith television series, played by Don Knotts. What was totally uncanny was that he even sounded like Barney Fife. We couldn't help cracking up.

But this was no laughing matter, so we finally put the governor on and regained our composure, knowing full well that this cocky little MP had the ability – and the temperament – to cause us some big-time headaches.

He took our full names, rank, military service numbers and units of command, and then told us to get our asses back to Bien Hoa Army Base. Like *yesterday*! He said we'd be hearing about this from our company commander. We headed out pronto, no questions asked. Within fifteen or twenty minutes another deuce and a half had stopped for us.

Noticing that the cab already had two troops, we were about to jump into the canvas-covered rear. But the troop in charge insisted they'd squeeze over and make room up front. As we drove up Highway 1 towards the base, we learned that the truck driver, a PFC, was a new replacement recruit and was being trained to take over as the new driver of this U.S. Army deuce and a half. He was actually in the process of being trained right then by the other guy, a short-timer specialist 4th class. The 4th class in charge happily let us know that he was flying home to the world on a freedom bird out of Bien Hoa Air Base in only five short days.

The PFC driver was having difficulty with the gears, which I thought was kind of funny. But in appreciation of the lift, I held my tongue. And wouldn't you know, my smart-ass friend Frenchie spoke up and said, "Hey private, why don't you grind me a few pounds while you're at it." No respect or appreciation whatsoever for the lift. What a screwball.

When we arrived at the base, just at dark, I turned to Frenchie and said, "Let's break loose with a few bucks for these guys." He dug into his fatigues and I did the same. They didn't want the dough, but I insisted. Generosity needs to be rewarded.

The next few days were edgy, because we expected the wrath of God to descend. Or at the very least, we expected to get bogged down in typical bureaucratic U.S. Army paperwork. Mercifully, it never happened. Our little Saigon AWOL incident apparently went unreported.

We'd lucked out. This time, anyhow.[1]

THE STREET IN SAIGON WHERE FRENCHIE AND I GOT NAILED BY THE HARD-NOSED MP

---

[1] Soldiers going AWOL during the height of the Vietnam War was greater than in any other conflict America had been involved in up until then.

FRENCHIE IN SAIGON RESTAURANT

FRENCHIE AND FELLOW TROOP AT BASE CLUB. PICTURE TAKEN
MOMENTS BEFORE OUR SAIGON AWOL ESCAPADE

WHO'S MY ENEMY?

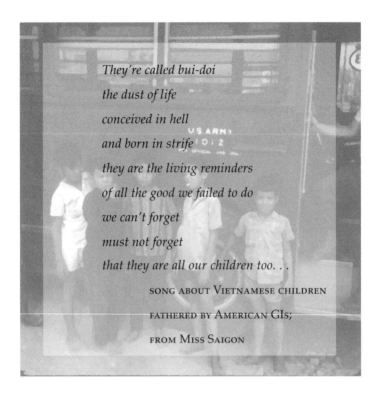

They're called bui-doi

the dust of life

conceived in hell

and born in strife

they are the living reminders

of all the good we failed to do

we can't forget

must not forget

that they are all our children too. . .

SONG ABOUT VIETNAMESE CHILDREN

FATHERED BY AMERICAN GIs;

FROM MISS SAIGON

THIS PICTURE WAS TAKEN FROM MY BUS OF THE AREA VERY NEAR
THE DANGEROUS WHOREHOUSE ESCAPADE.

INCIDENT IN BIEN HOA

FOR ONCE, MY WORK CAME FAIRLY EASY THIS DAY. I only had four or five stops in Long Binh before I returned to the base with an abnormally light load of new recruits from the 90th Replacement. After dropping them off I went down to the hooch to visit with my friend Wino. We were just lying around, listening to the radio, when low and behold, here came crazy Frenchie with a six-pack of lukewarm Schlitz beer.

"Hey guys, I'm in a real good mood this afternoon," said Frenchie, as he tossed each of us a beer. "My commander let me off early because I'm doin' such a damned good job."

I glanced at Wino and said, "He's givin' us a line of bullshit, don't ya think?"

"Damn straight, Bowman," Wino replied.

Then I looked over at Frenchie and said, "Well, that's great, you're in a good mood. Let's celebrate."

"Well heck, holy cow," he shot back, "We've got nothin' here to celebrate with, except this piss-warm beer and a bunch of sweaty, loser GIs. Let's go find some real action."

"Like what kind of action, Frenchie?" said Wino.

"In my book, there's only one kind of action. . . a good lookin' nude chick, smooth shaved legs, with a little Johnson's baby oil and to top it off, the sweet smell of a sexy knockout perfume. We may not get all of that here in Nam, but I do know of a place where we can get one hell of a head start, and that's surely not here in this stinkin' hooch. It's downtown Bien Hoa."

"No way, guys," said Wino, "I'm married!"

I turned to Wino and said, "I'm married too, but it sure ain't stoppin' me. My Godforsaken wife is cheatin' on me, so I don't really give a damn. And to top it off, she can't even fake it by writing a chickenshit note once in a while."

Frenchie grabbed his M16 and a couple of magazines and said, "Let's get out of here, Bowman."

Wino just shook his head.

Still chugging the lukewarm beer, we split the hooch and started searching for a ride down the hill to the city of Bien Hoa.

"Are you sure I don't need my M16?" I asked Frenchie.

"Forget it, Bus Boy, I've got ya covered. Let's go."

We stood out on the main road and finally caught a duce and a half. When we told the driver we were heading for Bien Hoa he said, "You guys are a bit crazy, aren't you, goin' down there after dark?"

By the time he dropped us off on the outskirts it was getting pretty dark, and I began to have second thoughts, especially hitting town without a weapon of my own. But once again Frenchie assured me everything would be all right. Here we go again, I thought, recalling our previous AWOL escapade with the MP in Saigon.

As we walked down the dark road into the city, I confided the incident to Frenchie about the disgruntled rebel hooch maid on the bus. "This bitch pulled a knife on me and threatened me with it," I told him. And I added that she'd made threats about getting her Viet Cong buddies to take me out if she didn't get her way.

"Bowman," he said, surprised, "Why the hell didn't you tell me about this sooner?"

"Because I'm not a hundred percent sure she had a Viet Cong connection, so I made a promise to myself not to tell a soul. I've been mentally screwed up since then, and I'm especially freaked about the possibility that I killed her."

"You really snuffed that damn gook?"

"I think so. I tried to break her neck and crush her skull on the ground just outside the bus door."

"Bowman, if I were in your shoes and some stinkin'-ass gook threatened me, regardless if they were a woman or a man, enemy or not, I'd have blown their damned head completely off and splattered their brains all over the damn place. And any other slant eyed son-of-a-bitchin' gook that got in my way and made a whisper of a threat to my life would've got the same – a big dose of M16 pills. We'll just have to be a little extra careful down here tonight. Once we get inside with the whores I'll stay real close by, just in case something goes down."

What a comforting thought. I didn't have a good feeling about this little venture. No way.

As we approached a dilapidated two-story building at the end of a small alleyway, Frenchie, in a whisper, said, "We're here, Bowman." He pointed to an open second story window. "We've gotta climb up the side of this wall to that open window," he added. I pondered. What a strange way to enter a whorehouse.

"Why in the hell are we climbing up there?"

"Because the front entrance isn't safe. It's much better

to go up through here. You'll see. Don't worry Bowman; I've got it handled. Let's get our asses up there and get some good stuff."

"Okay, whatever you say. You've been here before. But you go first, because I don't want that 16 of yours aiming at my ass. And by the looks of this woodwork, it surely won't handle the two of us at the same time."

We crawled up the half-broken lattice to the second story window, which was already open. Soon as we got in a pleasant-looking Vietnamese woman greeted us. Apparently the head honcho. Frenchie said he'd be in the next room over, and told me to "Just sit down and relax, and the madam will be back in a few minutes with a real nice, attractive gal for you."

"Relax?" Ha! That was about the farthest thing from my mind.

I sat there on this old sagging bed, just waiting. Within moments, I heard a baby start to cry across the room, but I couldn't see any baby. The flickering light from a small kerosene lamp on a crude, box-like table was the only illumination, and was rather dim. No wiring or light bulbs in this place. The baby continued to cry. Then I heard a second one start up. My curiosity got the best of me. I got up, went across the room and pulled back an old canvas cover hanging clear to the floor, over the box. Inside were two little children, maybe twelve to eighteen months of age. Right there in this small wooden box lined with military poncho material, sort of a tucked away place where people in the States might place small kittens or puppies. The kids were both nearly tow-headed blondes. No doubt fathered by previous GIs who'd come here for sex, just like us.

My first thought was that they might become frightened at the sight of me. But instead, on seeing me they both stopped crying and began to smile and coo, apparently soothed by my presence. I reached down and gently touched both their heads. One child, to my astonishment, grabbed and held onto my hand as if he wanted me to pick him up. I just stayed there, kneeling down, looking at these little Asian-American guys. I felt kind of sorry for them. In fact, I almost shed a tear.

Then I heard someone coming down the hallway, so I let the canvas cover down and quickly went back across the room to the bed and sat down. A terrific looking French-Vietnamese gal came in, sat down next to me and immediately started kissing and hugging me. It was nice to hold a woman that seemed to desire me, and she seemed very romantic. A loving and delightful sort of gal. Her pretty, olive-complexioned face seemed to glow in the dim and flickering light. The two kids inside the box didn't make a peep. For being so young, they were amazingly well trained; or, I should say, very disciplined.

My sexy companion began unbuttoning my fatigues. I then took off my jungle boots and trousers. I still had my fatigue shirt on, but it was completely unbuttoned. We began hugging and kissing, and I managed to slip all of her PJ style clothing off. We both seemed to really enjoy each other in a way that was different from the other Vietnamese women I'd been with.

After sex, we just lay on the bed, holding and caressing one another as if we were in love. Eventually, we sat up, holding each other and enjoying the moment and the mild and pleasant warmth of the evening.

As we watched the shadows playing across the walls and ceiling, I began to smell the distinct odor of weed. I assumed it was coming from the next room, where Frenchie was getting it on with his own gal. He was sort of a crazy lush and a gutsy kind of fellow, and did enjoy a pull on the wacky weed every now and then, so it wasn't unusual to catch him smoking a joint. Especially when he was around sexy women, or out of sight of the lifers.

Then I heard footsteps coming down the hall. They sounded like a man's boots. All the Vietnamese ladies wore light sandals or sometimes no shoes at all. As the unknown person got close to our room, I began to fear the worst. Maybe it was the enemy. A moment later, I heard a man's voice speaking in loud Vietnamese. Then all hell broke loose. A loud burst of gunfire echoed through the building; four to six rounds, I thought, maybe more. Two or more rounds came blasting through the wall into our room, scattering wood splinters in every direction. We both jumped off the bed and ran directly into a small, dark closet space that had a frayed, torn sheet-like material covering the doorway.

I was trembling from head to toe. What the hell was going on in the other room? With no weapon, I felt completely helpless and terribly vulnerable. My trousers were in my hands, but my jungle boots sat on the floor and my white boxer underwear was lying in plain sight on the dark blanket on the bed. This color contrast was like a bright neon sign. If a Viet Cong came in and spotted my boots or underwear, I'd be dead meat.

Then we heard scuffing around and more yelling. A Vietnamese woman's voice this time. Then several more shots rang out. I figured I was about to die. But I was frozen to the spot, scared to move for fear that I'd be seen or heard – and be the next to get snuffed!

Then a familiar voice rang out, "Bowman, are you okay?" It was my buddy Frenchie.

"Yes, I'm Okay!" I answered. I was so damn relieved to hear his voice. I had had visions of him crumpled on the floor, his chest shot full of holes.

CHRIS
The meat is cheap in Saigon
I used to love getting stoned, waking up with
some whore
I don't know why I went dead; it's not fun
anymore
KIM
I'm seventeen, and I'm new here today
The village I come from seems so far away
All of the girls know much more what to say
But I know
I have a heart like the sea
A million dreams are in me
CHRIS
Good Jesus, John, who is she?
AMERICANS (AND CROWD)
The Cong is tight'ning the noose
Is it a week or a day or an hour that we got?
Tonight could be our last shot got to put it to
use

FROM *MISS SAIGON*. LYRICS BY

RICHARD MALTY, JR AND ALAIN BOUBLIL

BUSY MARKETPLACE . . . DOWNTOWN BIEN HOA

"Get your butt in here right now," he hollered, "Hurry the hell up, you need protection."

Practically on the run, I slipped into my trouser fatigues, grabbed my boots and boxer shorts, and ran into his room – almost falling over a dead man in a large pool of blood in the doorway!

A Vietnamese woman, bleeding severely from her hip and lower leg and obviously in severe pain, lay groaning and squirming on the floor nearby. In the dim light of a kerosene lamp, I saw it was the madam he'd shot. My gal came in and leaned down to her, sobbing and saying something quietly in Vietnamese as she tried to console her.

This was no time to feel sorry. This was a time to preserve our lives and get the hell out of there. I looked down at the dead man and saw a rifle. I had to lift his arm to get it. It was an SKS, Chinese communist rifle. Clearly, the man was a Viet Cong.

Still half dressed, Frenchie and I raced for the open window we'd come in through. As we ran, I opened the bolt of the SKS carbine to see if it was loaded. It was. In fact, there was an unfired cartridge chambered into the breech. The VC guerrilla had meant business.

I leaned out the window and dropped my boots to the ground. We were two stories up and in one hell of a hurry. We needed to get our asses far away from there as quickly as possible. What a bitch it was, dark as holy hell.

I threw the frayed, well-used canvas sling of the SKS carbine over my shoulder, but the damn thing was real tight from having been in the possession of a small-framed Vietnamese. And I needed to free both hands to climb out the window and descend. From behind us, we could hear the two babies crying, frightened by the gunfire and the ruckus. Frenchie and I scooted out the window and scampered frantically down the dilapidated wooden lattice, praying that the flimsy thing wouldn't collapse before we reached the ground.

I picked up my boots on the run in the pitch dark. It's a damn wonder I could even find them. We ran like deer for half a mile or so, until we were both out of breath and my bare feet could stand no more torture. We stopped for a breather in a dark alley and I told Frenchie to keep an eye out while I put my boots on. My feet felt like they were on fire, but the adrenaline rush was so high that it didn't matter much. Frenchie and I jumped on the first truck that came by, and got our butts back to the base. And we swore we'd breathe not a word to anyone about our little AWOL incident in the city of Bien Hoa. And we didn't.

But I will forever remember those two small Asian-American children. It's as if I left a part of myself back there with those kids, and with the affectionate French-Vietnamese gal. Wild and crazy and as terrifying as the event was, those people touched my heart. And I will always wonder what kind of future they had, if they were able to survive in such a harsh and hostile environment.

To this day, it makes me sad to think of all the children fathered by U.S. soldiers, and left behind in Vietnam due to America's unfortunate and meaningless involvement in that tragic war.[1]

---

1 Estimates of the number of children fathered by American GIs during the Vietnam war range from as few as 15,000 to as many as 400,000. when the French withdrew in 1954, they transported 4,000 French Vietnamese children to be raised in France. During the final days of the war, Operation Babylift brought 3,300 Vietnamese children out of the country, bound for adoption with American, Canadian, European or Australian families.

WHO'S MY ENEMY?

SERIOUSLY PONDERING . . . WHAT THE HELL IS NEXT IN THIS DAMNED WAR?

SLIGHTLY DISGUSTED AND DEPRESSED - THE WAR IS HEADED NOWHERE.

MYSTERY IN OUR MINDS

*We grabbed our M-16 rifles and woke up the
rest of the unit. They*

*Fanned out into a perimeter around the radar
to repel any attackers*

*But luckily the action was concentrated on the
big artillery guns far*

*Away from our position. The Viet Cong had
breached our wire through*

*The floors of the shops and whorehouses that
had grown up around*

*That side of the base. So much for the "friendly"
mamasans with there*

Toothless grins!

Artilleryman Marshall Darling, on the website,

Rockets of Tet, Pictures and Poetry of the Vietnam War

ALTHOUGH SWORN TO SECRECY, Frenchie and I discussed our Bien Hoa adventure together frequently. We both agreed that the gun-toting gook that stormed into the whorehouse was definitely a Viet Cong guerrilla. Who else would've been armed with a fully loaded SKS, Chinese communist assault rifle?

It was common knowledge that guerrilla bandits came by these whorehouses and various other business establishments, especially the ones that were lucrative, to collect taxes. It was another form of coercion, harassment, and the stealing of hard-earned money from the civilian population. And a way for them to fund their cause, I suppose. Of course, this particular VC may have showed up at the boom boom parlor just to have sex. Or maybe he was a relation or boyfriend of one of the mamasans, just paying them a visit, and happened to run into us and acted accordingly – kill or be killed.

On the other hand, it could have been a full-blown trap, with the madam or one of the girls setting us up to have the Viet Cong come in and wipe me and Frenchie both out.

The real mystery was why in the world did the madam turn on Frenchie. Why, as soon as she saw the dead guerrilla lying on the floor, did she start yelling and screaming at the top of her lungs and swinging a machete (as Frenchie later claimed) in a manner designed to do great bodily harm? The madam, said Frenchie, had picked up this weapon from under a small bunk and had gone on a mad rampage. Maybe the dead man was a friend of hers, or a relative; that would certainly explain it. With the M16 still in his hands, Frenchie had instinctively sidestepped the irate madam and shot another burst of rounds into her lower extremities. Anyhow, that's the story he told me.

We discussed this incident in spyglass detail, over and over, trying to come up with a logical explanation of what had actually gone down. His Vietnamese gal, Frenchie said, had just gone downstairs to bring them both back some special Vietnamese tea concoction when the VC walked into the room. Frenchie decided that the whorehouse madam and his gal for the evening were both involved in some way with the enemy, voluntarily or not. The madam was the money collector for the establishment, and like it or not she had to go along with the Charlie's wishes or be snuffed out – or maybe suffer other terrible consequences. We were probably way out in left field in terms of what we figured, but in the end, it didn't matter. It was dirty water under a dangerous bridge.

"The hell with it, Frenchie," I finally said, "Who gives a rats ass? We're not the friggin' FBI, nor do we need to be. We came out of there alive, we're here talking about it, and that's all that really counts. Let's just forget about the whole damn thing." And that's where it ended between us.

But not for me. Over the next several weeks I replayed the ordeal over and over in my head. I never brought the subject up to Frenchie again, just kept it to myself. And I was probably over reacting. Still, the tape kept playing. But after this hair-raising incident, our enthusiasm for going AWOL again was definitely dampened down. In fact, our rambunctious and crazy shenanigans came to a screeching halt.

Another thing: I got the impression that Frenchie's little story about shooting the Vietnamese madam was most likely somewhat tainted. While I can't prove that he was lying about the shooting, I did conclude that he was so frightened for his life when he shot the VC guerrilla that on top of that, when the madam, for whatever she had going on her mind, started chewing him out with her loud, abusive language and aggressive behavior, he basically panicked and over reacted. I should know. I was in the adjacent room, listening to the ruckus, and gunfire, and trembling in fear of my life. I mean, maybe she was simply freaked that something like this had gone down in her place, and the idea that someone would blow someone else away made her act without thinking.

When I had run into Frenchie's dimly lit room, side-stepping the dead Viet Cong, I never did see the long knife or machete Frenchie kept insisting he'd seen. The only weapon I actually saw was the SKS Chinese carbine lying beside the dead communist soldier. True, the room was only lit with a kerosene lamp the same as in mine, and the light was pretty dim. The machete could easily have been lying around in the semi-dark, or had possibly fallen under one of the old beds, but I didn't actually see it. At that nerve-racking moment, neither Frenchie nor I were interested in anything but self-preservation. So, the way I figure it, if he made up a little white lie about the madam swinging a machete around just to intensify the situation and to make the entire shooting incident seem more realistic and justifiable, so be it.

Something obviously pulled his chain for him to fire additional M16 rounds into the madam. After rethinking the entire incident, I came to one final conclusion: unless you stood in your comrade's boots – a virtual impossibility – no soldier can sit back and judge or disrespect what another soldier does in an intense, terrifying situation like that.

Regardless of what exactly went down that frightful evening in the city of Bien Hoa, I'll never condemn or hold my good friend Frenchie liable for any wrongdoing. I'll stand strong and firm behind his judgment. Whether or not a machete or an elongated knife was involved, Frenchie convinced me beyond the shadow of a doubt that he acted accordingly, in terms of the life threatening and horrifying situation he was presented with. In time of war, when a comrade is in sheer terror for his life that's all that a buddy can really expect.

THAT'S ME, WITH PFC ETTLEMAN AND PFC FLETCHER

WHO'S MY ENEMY?

MISS LEE, WITH A GROUP OF HOOCH MAIDS LAYING SANDBAGS AROUND A HOOCH

WHO'S MY ENEMY?

*I just need somewhere to dump all my
negativity*

VAN MORRISON

Our leaders, our leaders

Our leaders is what they always say,

But it's bullshit, it's bullshit

It's bullshit they feed us every day. . .

SONG OF THE 35TH TACTICAL FIGHTER WING AT

PHAN RANG, VIETNAM

THE VIETNAMESE GUERRILLAS forced the American soldiers to live in constant fear and paranoia as the guerrillas repeatedly displayed their brutal ingenuity.

We faced mostly local VC, peasants armed with World War II rifles and no heavy weapons. They were taking on the best army in the world . . . . We respected them from day one . . . they always hit us where we were the weakest. They always decided when, where, and how to fight us; on what terrain and under what conditions. They did an awful lot with an awful little . . . . We all knew they were poor, not stupid from the website, *lifeisannoying.com*

It was getting to me; fury about what I was sure Karen was into back home, the business about trying

117

to smuggle the weapons, the AWOL trip to Saigon, and finally the AWOL whorehouse incident at Bien Hoa. Between all these, and losing sleep over whether or not the Viet Cong had been sicked on me because of the incident with that rebel mamasan on the bus in downtown Bien Hoa, I was a nervous wreck.

During my travels to pick up and deliver the hooch maids, I'd often run smack-dab into mass congestion on the narrow streets of Bien Hoa. Due to the large numbers of villagers and peasants, the streets and alleys would be a sea of people, all going about their normal chores, marketing goods, whatever.

The streets were like a can of sardines, and if I didn't keep the bus moving I'd be screwed. If I'd stopped dead in the middle of that mass of stubborn little people, God have mercy. It would be like dropping a crippled grasshopper into the middle of a nest of army ants and then expecting it to escape. No damn way.

Once, I actually got caught up like that, had a hell of a time moving again, and vowed never to repeat the experience – even if it meant running over some of the villagers. As luck would have it, and only by sheer accident, I don't think I ever actually injured any Vietnamese seriously. But on several occasions I came within a whisker. Once or twice, I probably sideswiped a peasant or two.

Usually, I'd shift down, blast the horn and cruise at a slow speed (especially when faced with mass congestion) but never stop. Never! If I ran over one parked bicycle, I must have run over at least a hundred. I raised hell with the crowds, mashing bikes, trashing a few cyclo carts, tipping over and busting up market tables, and muddying up many a Vietnamese during the rainy, monsoon season.

It got to be an everyday occurrence to smash something or spew out muck or muddy water over the crowds of peasants and townspeople determined to occupy the roads and streets in and around Bien Hoa. I'd never stop. Many times, I'd look into my rearview mirrors shortly after a mishap and see a sea of fists shaking and cursing me. And smashing a bike or a cart, or having all those people angry with me freaked me out even more. Careless as I was, these incidents only set me on edge more, and intensified my fears of the unseen enemy.

The villagers were a very busy people, preoccupied with their daily routines and chores and accustomed to a culture that was somewhat primitive compared to ours. While they could tolerate the usual cyclist or papasan peddling a cyclo cart down their packed streets, our bulky American-made, big square-nosed military buses upset everything, including their patience. And I have to admit that my attitude didn't help. Though at the time, with fear and mental fatigue pressing in, I didn't see any other choice for my behavior.

One morning, the whole business about the rebel mamasan who I'd clubbed with my M16 then boot-stomped, came back to haunt me. I was in the city of Bien Hoa, picking up my regular hooch maids. My friend and translator, Miss Lee, climbed into the bus and whispered, "I have something I want to tell you." I told her to wait until the maids were on and the loud chatter had quieted down; their Vietnamese lingo was always magnified as they searched for seats.

By the time I shut the bus door and started back down the congested road to the base, the noise had calmed down enough, so I turned slightly to Lee and said, "Good morning, Lee, what did you want to tell me?"

"There is talk goin' around village that Cong have dolla on you," she said, almost whispering.

The blood rushed to my head. "Are you sure of that?" I asked.

She said, "Maybe just talk."

She began to act a little nervous, and I noticed that she kept looking back at some of the other hooch maids. Why, I didn't know.

Then Lee said, "No more talk, okay, you drive bus." She clammed up, as if someone or something was bothering her, so I dropped the subject.

As the hooch maids got off the bus at the base and shuffled off to their jobs I told Lee, "Have a nice day," but I didn't press her about this so-called Cong threat.

Now, I became even more concerned. I wasn't sure if what Lee had said was bullshit, or whether it had to do with the rebel hooch maid I tried to kill. I wanted to talk to Lee about it, but sensed that I had to be careful. Over the next few days, I noticed that she deliberately avoided me as much as possible. Something was all screwed up, and I didn't have a clue how to solve it.

I really needed this kind of news. (Not!) It was bad enough that I was grieving over my wife, now I had this damn black cloud hanging around. Did the VC want my ass or what? Sure they wanted me, I was in a war! My mind began to wander in complete despair.

The pressure kept building, and my effort to stay alert for danger became ever so numbing. All I could think of was getting snuffed out when I least expected it. Maybe driving through the overcrowded streets of Bien Hoa.

I began suspecting every villager or field peasant. I wanted to trust these people, but something kept telling me that danger was near, be aware, keep alert. Each day I'd make eye contact with some Vietnamese in black-clad pajamas working a rice paddy or truck garden. To me, they all looked sneaky and suspicious. Were they Viet Cong, or just disgruntled? Friend or foe? I'd look at an irritable ARVN soldier and wonder if he was actually on our side.

Christ, I thought, I didn't volunteer for this hell-hole war. I had refused to enlist, but had the "honor" of being drafted. (For a two-year active duty hitch and four more years of inactive service.) Government-issue dog tag number U.S. 568-33-707.

"Your dog tag number is your life now," my drill sergeant back in basic at Fort Lewis, Washington had said, "So don't ever forget it." He was right; I remember it to this day.

Dog tag number or whatever, who the hell cared about me or any other American serviceman over here in Vietnam? That's what I thought, becoming more and more bitter. My disrespectful government didn't give a damn. My mind dwelt on those Godforsaken asshole politicians and officials that had dropped us off in this pigsty, this disease-infested place. Most of those fat, cigar-chomping bastards were probably sitting down in their lush living rooms right now, sipping cocktails or champagne and watching the war on their color TVs. The sons-of-bitches could sleep easy tonight in their plush beds, now that they'd heard the "whole truth" from some "News at Ten" anchorman. The newscaster had let the entire American nation know that the enemy has sustained "Very heavy loses, with very few loses among our American serviceman." "Progress," they'd call it.

Tell the public what they want to hear, tell them what sounds appealing. Additionally, the newsman certainly reported, "Our boys can finally rest easy. The military sees some light down the tunnel, and it's just a matter of time before American involvement will finish the war."

What an immense crock of bullshit!

Disease was everywhere in this mosquito-infested land. Especially in the smaller rural villages. Malaria and tuberculosis were common. Hepatitis, skin infections and parasitic diseases were everywhere, mostly caused by bathing in, and, or consuming water containing human or animal feces. If only the Vietnamese had been provided with washing soap and taught the value of using it.

Vietnam was also a cesspool of local government corruption. Anyone or anything could be bought for a price. Literally. Corruption among South Vietnamese troops, NVA/VC troops, American troops and the civilian population was rampant. Hard work and honest effort by most of the South Vietnamese was going completely to waste because of a few corrupt, greedy bastards willing to sell their country down the drain for a few measly dollars.[1]

Corruption was an enemy within the government. It violated honest people's efforts and their hope for fair treatment. The hard working people of South Vietnam, who were the majority, didn't deserve this festering cancer that had been generated by a few of their own self-centered people.

The more I thought about it, the more I thought that South Vietnam was doomed from the start of the war. Communism seemed likely to prevail.

Nor, I thought, were the Viet Cong, who were a mainstay of the National Liberation Front, any better.

---

[1] Some estimates had it that one fifth of South Vietnam's annual budget was raked off the top in Saigon and either sent to overseas banks or used to finance businesses.

122

Their tactics found them occasionally booby-trapping school grounds, and sometimes a church or a worship courtyard. The bastards killed, maimed and tortured innocent school children as a way to terrorize the South Vietnamese who cooperated with the Americans. On a few occasions, female teachers were tortured and raped in public demonstrations. These despicable acts were a symbol and mainstay of the extreme power the Communist Party had. The VC had a bag of nasty, vicious and horrible tricks. While I don't know if this was official VC/NVA policy, and was perhaps carried out by isolated units, it was certainly going on. Just like the rampant corruption among South Vietnamese officials.

"All's fair in love and war" seemed to be the rule. Not by me. This was as if the "devil's daughter" was in bed with the Charlies, and I found it disgraceful.

All this, the reports I heard, the things I experienced, turned me more and more into a bitter, disgruntled and terrified human being. I hated the feeling but didn't know how to escape. I simply had to wait it out and hope I'd make it.

When I picked up new replacement recruits in Long Binh, especially after dark, I became extra cautious. The firefights between the NVA/VC and ARVN and American troops were intensifying again, especially after dark in the Cong Paddies area and out near the big Bien Hoa Air Base. Inside, I was a nervous wreck, but still managed to fake an outer composure. I tried to concentrate on my job but this got increasingly harder, because my mind kept going back to the incident on the bus with the rebel hooch maid.

Finally, I got a chance to talk to Lee about the supposed VC threat. She tried to convince me that it was only a rumor, but at the same time she also said I needed to be extremely careful and not do anything stupid anymore.

What the hell did that mean? I was still very confused.

When I asked Lee again if this threat had anything to do with the rebel hooch maid, and whether she'd recovered from the frenzied beating I had given her, Lee simply clammed up, acting as though she hadn't heard me. When I pressed her she became flustered and said, "No talk, no talk," and left in a hurry. This sudden evasive behavior was deeply troubling. I'd always regarded Miss Lee as a good and reliable friend, but her abrupt change in attitude had me confused and soon began to drive me nuts.

I was falling apart at the seams. I could only hope that this would soon blow over. But my trust in mankind was dwindling, and the distinct line between ordinary Vietnamese and who the enemy was, had become a hazy gray. Nothing was definite anymore. I decided to trust no one, not even the village children.

As if my nerves weren't jangled enough, one morning as I was driving down one of the jammed Bien Hoa streets I heard a loud series of pop, pop, pop, like small arms fire. I almost came unglued. I grabbed my M16 – which always lay on the dash by the front windshield – and slammed a round into the chamber. I jerked open the bus door and peered out, looking at the villagers, wondering where the shooting had came from. Two elderly mamasans just stood there, very calm, tending to their chores. Both were washing and rinsing cloths in a crude tub. Almost immediately, I began to feel like a fool; a group of village children had been playing in a small side alleyway just off the main drag. They'd set off a cluster of loud firecrackers resembling rapid gunfire. And that was it. I smiled graciously and waved to the two elderly mamasans and drove off. They probably had a great laugh.

Occasionally, I'd take a soda pop on the bus with me, and after I finished the drink would place the empty on the dashboard, near my M16. Generally, a hooch maid or one of the village kids would ask me for the empty, and I'd gladly give it to them. But when I learned that the Viet Cong would take empty beer and soda cans and use them as casings for homemade hand-grenades, I stopped that practice in a major hurry. Making damn sure to crush the cans flat, I'd put them in one of my fatigue pockets. My survival, I decided, depended on being very suspicious and super cautious of almost anything and everything. And everyone! A horrible trait, but one I found difficult to set aside.

If it wasn't one end, it was the other. My body was rebelling, mentally and physically. The mess hall chow tasted like crap, and I had the trots. One day, after picking up recruits at the 90th Replacement, I started experiencing severe abdominal discomfort. The pain got so damn excruciating that I had to pull over. I grabbed my canteen, split from the bus and ran across the road for a clump of elephant grass and tall reeds on the edge of a vast rice paddy, in plain sight of several distant Vietnamese peasants. With no toilet paper (made sure to carry a supply after that!) I used the canteen to scoop up water and clean myself.

Back on the bus, the new recruits didn't say a single word. They just watched, probably wondering what the hell was wrong. Their first day in Nam and their driver's got the trots. And it didn't end there. The trots kept coming back. My trips to the dispensary were almost as frequent as getting out of my bunk in the morning. The army doctors took test samples: Urine, stool, blood, and temperature. They probed and poked, and scratched their heads in despair.

Meanwhile, I was losing weight like a son-of-a-bitch, while these cocky young Army doctors walked around the meat shop, sporting their damned white lab coats with stethoscopes dangling over their shoulders, and scratching their asses for lack of anything better to do.

Some days were better than others, and I longed for the day when I could get out of this hellhole of Vietnam. Alive, if I could just hang on long enough.

Who was my enemy? I kept wondering. Was it only the Viet Cong and the NVA? That disgruntled ARVN soldier supposedly on our side? That peasant farmer over in the rice paddy who looked up and grinned as I drove past? The bastard lifer officers and NCOs? The whole stupid war? My own government? My unfaithful wife? Or just the army grub?

Damn hard to maintain your composure when you're constantly wondering.

WASH DAY, VIETNAMESE FASHION

WHO WAS MY ENEMY? I KEPT WONDERING.

WHO'S MY ENEMY?

NEW REPLACEMENT RECRUITS - THEY'VE BEEN IN-COUNTRY LESS THAN 48 HOURS.
A VERY CLOSE CALL. TELLING SIGNS OF AN ENEMY ROCKET OR RPG THAT REARRANGED
THE LEFT REAR BUMPER OF MY BUS AND BLEW OUT MY REAR TIRE AT THE SAME TIME.

FIREFIGHT AT CONG PADDIES

*Life is a tragedy when seen in close-up, but a
comedy in long shot.*

CHARLIE CHAPLIN

OVER SEVERAL MONTHS, my fellow driver Rory and
I delivered thousands and thousands of new replacement troops to their duty stations in Long Binh. The
stops varied, day by day. On one day I'd have a light
load of half a dozen recruits, on another, forty or more. I
often thought about what might be the final destiny for
these guys. Would they end up on a pleasant lift back to
the world in one of those comfortably plush seats on a
707 freedom bird, waited on by a sweet-smelling, good
looking, round-eyed flight attendant? Or would their
journey back to there loved ones involve a grim trip on
a cargo plane, stuffed away in a reusable light aluminum box – a temporary coffin?

This particular day started out normally. A fairly
large group awaited me for transport to the Bien Hoa
Army Base. As usual, I announced over the microphone, "Troops assigned to the 537th Personnel Service
Company in processing, report and file in at window
number three." (I always made this announcement at
least twice, sometimes more, depending on the number
of recruits.)

Prior to the announcement, many of the recruits, all
decked out in their newly issued jungle fatigues, had

already begun to form a line at my window. In general, it was a privilege working and transporting these guys. They were usually courteous, with a solid respect for the seasoned soldier in Vietnam. As they fell out to get their duffel bags and started loading into the bus, a new recruit approached me; a PFC. He was polite, and maybe even a bit shy.

"Do you have a moment sir?" he asked.

"Sure do," I replied, "But you don't need to call me 'sir.' I'm not an officer, just a regular army grunt, like you."

"I understand, but I hope you can help me find out some information. After what I saw and heard last night, I'm scared to death."

"What happened?"

"Many of us new guys were assigned to a big barracks for the night," said the private. "And at about 0200 hours this morning, all hell broke loose. The enemy – I guess they call them "Congs" or "Charlies" – started blasting away at us. All kinds of small arms fire, mortars, rockets, the works."

"Did anybody get hit or killed?" I asked.

"I don't think so. I'm not real sure of that, but it sure raised hell with everybody. And I know one thing for sure: I was scared shitless. First time in my life I've ever had someone try to blow my head off."

I said, "Don't take it personal, the Charlies were not specifically trying to kill you new guys, they were just trying to inflict general chaos, and you happened to be lucky enough to be in the middle of it."

"Well," he went on, "Regardless of what those Charlies were up to, we were all rattled. None of us in the barracks were hit, but two or three rockets or mortars hit just outside. One landed in the corner of our complex and scattered sand and sand bags to hell and gone, and another got an unmanned deuce and a half just a few yards away. Shortly after that, we heard a massive blast of rapid machine gun fire from some American helicopters."

"That's fairly normal around here," I said. "Charlie likes to let us know he's still out there."

The private asked me if I thought his chances were good of making it out of Vietnam alive with an infantry (MOS). I looked at him sympathetically then said, "Well, I'm not God, so I really can't say. It all depends on where you'll be stationed and what assignments you get."

He said, "Most likely I'll be assigned to some kind of infantry, grunt outfit. I guess you call 'em front line ground pounders. Some buck sergeant back in California told me that my chances were from slim to none of gettin' out of Vietnam alive."

"At Fort Ord Army Base?"

"Yes, sir."

"Forget the 'sir,' crap."

"I'm sorry, Mr. Bowman, we just talk like that down south in Alabama. We show respect to our elders, and anyone of knowledge and authority, if you know what I mean. I was brought up to show respect to others or my pa would whip us."

I said, "I totally understand, but did you say that a bastard, brain-dead buck sergeant told you that you wouldn't make it out of here in once piece?"

He nodded and replied, "He told all the trainees in my platoon the same damn thing."

"Sort of the same thing happened to me up at Fort Lewis, Washington," I told him. "That pisses me off to the max. That cocky, dumb–ass buck sergeant's commanding officer should know about this crap. He needs to be tightened up, or maybe they should even shit-can the son-of-a-bitch. On the other hand, his commanding officer is probably some lifer bastard that wouldn't give a damn anyway. Maybe even condones this outrageous behavior. I guess the Army needs a few dimwit token sergeants to fill the dumb jobs. Take it from me, that stupid, three striper dunce-cap probably can't find a good job anywhere else in this man's world, so that's why he's a lifer buck sergeant in the United States Army. He's probably failed at every other respectable job he's had, and now the son-of-a-bitch has got some real buck sergeant mentality and authority, so he picks on you privates and PFCs to get his jollies. That really takes a lot of intelligence, doesn't it?"

The private smiled. "You're exactly right," he said, "I sure don't think it was very bright of him to say those things."

"Don't worry about the army bullshit. And take it from me, you'll see plenty more of it."

Then I said, "I'll shut up for a while, makes me pissed off and sick just to talk about it. I just can't stand lifer bullshit, arrogance and ignorance." Then I had a thought. "Say," I went on, "Can you cook up a good meal or push papers at all?"

"What do you mean, push papers?"

"I mean, can you finger a typewriter and office work and such?"

"Hell, no," he said, "I've never touched a typewriter or nothing like that. Where I come from, that kind of stuff is for girls, sissies and faggots."

"Oh it is, is it?" I said, laughing. "Well, that being the case, can you cook up a meal?"

"Hell, yeah, I used to be one of the head cooks for our church cookouts back home in Alabama. I can cook up almost anything."

"Well that's great," I said. "So here's something to think about: when you get to your infantry outfit, the very first thing you need to do is somehow let your commanding officer know that you're one hell of a good cook. I've heard through the grapevine that good cooks are generally in demand. And by the way, don't let any SOB tell ya you need a cook's MOS for the slot. That's the best advice I can give you."

He said, "Sounds like a real good plan to me. Thanks for the skinny."

"No problem at all, good luck, and keep your head down. Now let's get the hell out of here," I said, and I climbed into the bus for the trip to Bien Hoa Army Base.

As I drove out of Long Binh from the 90th Replacement, I thought to myself, now what the hell did I know, I was only one pay-grade in rank above a PFC. But I sure hope my advice helps him make it through OK.

Then I went back to concentrating on my job, getting this full busload safely delivered. By now it was late afternoon, and because of the increased number of new recruits it had taken a lot more time to process them through and get them all loaded than I'd expected. I'd had maximum loads before, but this one was more time consuming, due mainly to some paperwork bottleneck.

On a few previous trips, the Charlies had tried to take me out, along with my bus – generally with light arms fire from AK47's and SKS rifles. If they attacked, it usually took place at dusk or shortly thereafter. And the sun had already gone down.

Enormous stretches of rice paddies, water dikes and truck gardens stretched out along both sides of the road we were on. Generally, because of the presence of so many peasants, civilian farmers and the ARVN and American troops, the Charlies would stay back in thicker cover during daylight hours. But after dark it was another story. Darkness was their ally. I sometimes think they had night vision, like cats. And as sneaky as a pack of raccoons.

On this particular trip, I had two main concerns. My first was this: on previous trips I'd noticed the bus's engine had begun to act up. This was a diesel, and I believed that the trouble was most likely caused by one or two faulty fuel injectors or a dirty fuel filter. Or maybe both.

My second concern was the Charlie Congs. And I didn't want to delay, because one of my fears was already becoming real: darkness was setting in fast, and I was barely out of Long Binh. I now had to turn my headlights on. But for now at least, the bus' engine seemed to be running perfectly. I crossed my fingers.

By the time I was midway on my route, it was pitch black. I couldn't see off to my right or left or behind and we were rapidly approaching the area called Cong Paddies. As I continued to drive, and wasting as little time as possible, I noticed distant streaks of colored lights and flashes crossing the road up ahead. The concentration was massive. At this point I became very concerned, I recognized these streaks of light, and it wasn't good news. These were tracer rounds being fired, more than likely a combined effort of both NVA and Viet Cong forces, with ARVN and American forces returning fire.

The firefight appeared to be widespread and well organized. Red streaks of tracer bullets and green and yellow streaks from light arms-fire poured in from both sides of the roadway; friendly fire from cobra gun ships and enemy fire from quad-50's. White spotlights from our American observation choppers swept back and forth across the scene. This was a massive array of firepower going on just ahead. Far from a good situation. My gut was churning, and I began to get a very eerie feeling. It seemed as if the enemy was on one side of the road and the ARVN and American forces were on the other. And we were *on* the road, approaching this hellhole dead on. I slowed the bus to a crawl, then eventually to a complete stop. At the same time, I turned to my load of recruits and yelled, "Get down, get down! Lie as flat as you can on the floor and for Christ's sake stay down!"

The firefight up ahead was so intense, I was convinced that we had no way of getting through without being torn apart. What a hell of a decision; do I make a mad dash and try to get through that maze of firepower? Do I just stay put? Or what? In that damn war, you were more likely to get whacked by the enemy, but in a situation like this friendly fire could do you in just as easily.

I thought about finding a place to turn the bus around and get my guys the hell away from this death trap. One big-ass problem, however: the bus was so damn long and the drop off at the sides was so sudden that it was virtually impossible to turn the sucker around. The roadway resembled a river-road levee with steep embankments, high enough to stay above the periodic flooding during monsoons, but not wide enough to turn around on.

The roadway was already soaking wet from an earlier downpour, and if I tried to turn around and it slipped off the mucky shoulders, it would be curtains for us all. But I had to do something fast, I couldn't just sit there.

We were incredibly vulnerable, parked stone dead on the road in the pitch dark, and with the damned bus lit up like a Christmas tree.

Plus which, I had a major knot in my stomach.

I continued looking into the rear view mirrors for any sign of approaching enemy. Then, just as I decided to move the bus forward in search of a wide space where we might turn around, a different squad of Charlies, who had apparently been hiding in the darkness of the rice paddies, cut loose on us with a barrage of small arms fire. Judging from the appearance and direction of their tracers, they were still quite a way out in the paddy. Good thing I had decided to move; if they'd been any closer we'd have had it. With only an M16 and a 45 for protection, we'd have been no match. I firmly believe that if I hadn't started moving the bus forward when I did, we would've been toast. Dead meat. Slaughtered, or at least captured.

Miraculously, we got out of that first attack without a scratch. But now we were headed into a second barrage of both enemy and friendly fire. I had no choice now, I couldn't turn back and I couldn't stay, because the other Charlies were right on our ass. This was not a healthy situation. We had to get out of there. And fast!

My foot went to the floor on the accelerator. "Go baby go!" I yelled, hoping this son-of-a-bitchin' engine wouldn't quit on us now. I shouted out again to the new recruits, "Stay down, stay down!" By now, I was going sixty. I clenched my teeth and tensed up out of shear panic. Here we go again. The night sky was lit up like the 4th of July. All kinds of tracer rounds streaking in front of me, overhead, behind, right flank and left flank. Enemy fire or friendly fire, at this point, I didn't know and didn't care which was coming from where. "Let us get through, please let us get through," was my prayerful thought.

By now I had a full head of steam, and we were through the heaviest part of the firefight. But as I carried on, I suddenly saw massive chunks of pavement scattered over the entire road, and a large blasted hole consuming a good portion of my right lane. An enemy rocket or maybe a RPG had hit the road. I was brought up short, stunned by the sudden appearance of the crater. But I had to go for it. I swerved to the left, trying to avoid the large cavity and most of the larger chunks. We were lucky. Well, almost lucky; I missed the entire hole but in the process we practically slid off the left side of the road, nearly tipping the bus over. When I swerved so quickly, the bus began to slide and tip and at one point the steering wheel spun in my hands, almost breaking one of my thumbs. We had nearly cleared the maze of crap and debris, when I heard a loud bang, and the rear end of the bus started to bounce. For a moment, though I wasn't really sure, I thought we'd been hit with a round. The engine sputtered a few times but everything else seemed fine, so I continued speeding toward Bien Hoa Army Base. With my fingers crossed, praying that the engine would hold out long enough to get us there.

By now, I was beginning to feel more confident and the nervous tension began to subside. We pretty much had it made, I thought. In fact I was reasonably sure, because I could finally see the lights of Bien Hoa, now only a couple miles away. With all my cursing the military for their damn waste and incompetence, right now I was deliriously happy, and gratefully appreciative, to see those wonderful U.S. Army lights; my home, my castle, my palace of safety and security. For now at least, this was the best there was. It was my life.

WHO'S MY ENEMY?

I looked back at my load of recruits, half of them back in their seats by now and the other half, still a bit reluctant to get up, partially on the floor. Tremendously relieved and almost ecstatic, I yelled out, "We made it, we made it, guys!" A few of them clapped and cheered with relief.[1]

In my rearview mirrors I noticed a flashing red light rapidly approaching. I slowed to a stop, as a damned MP in a jeep pulled up in back of me. After taking his sweet-ass time dicking-off behind the bus, he walked up to the door side with his flashlight burning. As I opened the door he put one foot up on the first step, shined his blinding flashlight directly into my eyes, then climbed up and stood on the second step and scanned the recruits with his light.

"I see you've got one hell of a load of troops on the bus tonight," he said.

"Yes, I do!"

"What's your name, troop?"

"Specialist Ivan Bowman."

The MP says, "Well, Bowman, do you realize that you have one rear tire blown completely out?"

"No," I replied, "I wasn't aware of any flat tire."

"Now listen here, Bowman," he shot back, "Do you realize that you jeopardized your entire load of troops and yourself back there?"

"What are you talking about?"

"You know exactly what I'm talking about; you were using excessive speed."

---

[1] Following this incident, I had the privilege of cleaning up the vomit of several terrified new recruits.

"Yes," I answered, "I was speeding a bit back there. For one simple reason: I had to get through a serious firefight with a couple squads of Cong guerrillas."

About this time, one of my recruits inside the bus stood up and yelled out, "Hey you stupid-ass pig, there's no damn place for pigs in a firefight or any war zone. Go the hell back to the real world and pork somebody there! Did you want all of us to get our asses blown off?"

The recruit that spoke up was a SP/5, "specialist fifth class." I assumed he was well-seasoned, most likely on his second tour, since nobody else would've had the balls to say something like that. Including me. The MP glared back at the SP/5 recruit, and said, "I could write you up for using abusive language and disorderly conduct to a military policeman."

"Look," I quickly interjected, trying to divert the MP's attention to me, "I speeded up to keep from getting caught in a firefight. I didn't think it was a catastrophe to speed up in order to get away from a death trap. I wasn't going that fast in the first place. This is a war you know, not a damn kiddie's playground. I made a judgment call, and I feel I acted appropriate to the situation."

"Sorry, Bowman," replied the thickheaded MP, "I'm writin' you up on this one. Take it up with your company commander."

This totally pissed me off. I figured I'd catch hell from my company commander, and especially First Sergeant Bruno, when they heard about this stupid speeding ticket.

As I delivered the recruits to in processing many of them shook my hand and thanked me for doing what they thought was the right thing. Some expressed their dislike for the bastard MP for writing me up.

Later, I told my commanding officer, Captain Perry (the 537th PSC's new officer in charge of processing) about the enemy firefights and the flat tire on the back of the bus.

"Sounds like you were real lucky to get through that mess with only a flat tire," he said.

"Sir, we almost got our asses blown to hell. I didn't realize there was a squad of Charlie guerrillas practically sitting in our lap down near Cong Paddies. I would say sir, that if I hadn't put the bus in gear and gotten the hell down the road and out of there when I did, the enemy squad could've run through us like butter."

"How many Charlies do you think there were?" asked Captain Perry.

"Well, that's fairly hard to say for sure, especially in the dark, but if I was to guess, Cap, by the appearance of the tracers and the sounds of the quads and the light arms-fire that they dispersed, maybe a dozen Charlies in the first firefight, and at least double that or maybe more in the second barrage."

Captain Perry looked at me for a moment, thinking deeply, then said, "Bowman, here's the plan. I'm going to give you an armed convoy escort from here to Long Binh and back until those damn guerrilla units calm down. A jeep front and rear of the bus, and when I can get the manpower together, I'll throw in a deuce and a half, manned with at least four M16s. Each jeep will be equipped with a driver and passenger with M16s, and a manned M-60 caliber machine gun with plenty of ammo. All the troops will wear complete combat gear, with mandatory flak jackets."

"Sir, do you want me to wear complete combat gear in the bus?" I said.

"Yes, Bowman,"

"Sir, I don't want to disobey your order, but it does seem to be a little unfair to all the new replacement recruits."

"How's that?"

"Well, sir, I don't feel comfortable wearing all that combat gear, especially the flak jacket, when my new recruits don't have any protection other than the clothes they've got on their backs. If it's okay with you sir, I'd prefer not wearing my flak jacket. I'd rather stay on an equal basis with the guys I transport. They deserve that much, sir."

"Bowman, I'll leave that up to your discretion," replied the captain. "Now, when you're about to load up at the 90th, give me a call on the landline and I'll send out the armed jeep escorts to meet you at a rendezvous point well past the Cong Paddies area. Say, how's about Water Buffalo Corners, in that wide area of the road?"

"Sounds real good to me, sir!"

"Be sure and wait at Water Buffalo Corners if the escort is a bit late. I don't want you taking any more chances. And another thing: I've changed my mind on you not wearing combat gear. Look at it this way, Bowman, if the enemy takes you out because you're not wearing your flak jacket then you've jeopardized your entire load of new recruits, and we wouldn't want that, would we? So wear the damn thing."

"Sir, that does make a lot of sense. By the way, sir, did you ever get a diesel mechanic to check out that diesel problem on the bus, yet?"

"Damnit, Bowman," he said, a bit annoyed with himself, "I promised you I'd get on that a week ago, didn't I? I'll get on it first thing tomorrow morning. And I'll have the blown tire replaced too, guaranteed."

"Thanks a lot, sir!"

WHO'S MY ENEMY?

Although I didn't tell Captain Perry about the MP and the speeding ticket, I figured he'd find out about it soon enough. He was a decent guy and had a lot hanging on his shoulders, with all the new replacement recruits that we'd run through the process every day. I never worried too much about Captain Perry's ability to take charge. On the other hand, the crap that came down from the company commander's and first sergeant's office was unbelievable. Those two lifer bastards, together, as leaders, wouldn't have made a serious pimple on a good soldier's ass.

Another day in Vietnam. Another day of survival. As I crashed for the night, I found myself wondering if that infantry troop from down in Alabama would make it.

A WELL-ARMORED CONVOY. ROAD BETWEEN LONG BINH
AND BIEN HOA ARMY BASES

Major bombing and firefight just below our berm and concertina wire

Six ubiquitous Bell UH-1 "Huey" choppers in the process of raking the jungle pockets and hideouts of enemy NVA and Viet Cong forces with merciless firepower

Reinforcement troops brought in to help protect the perimeters of both Bien Hoa Army Base and Bien Hoa Air Base from the constant onslaught of relentless NVA and Viet Cong troops. Post-TET 1969

SHORT MAN'S SYNDROME

Military justice is to justice what military music is to music.

GROUCHO MARX

FIVE DAYS AFTER I was ticketed by the stubborn, heavy-handed MP for speeding, I got the unpleasant news to report to the first sergeant's office.

First Sergeant Bruno was a lifer and a son-of-a-bitch. He ate, slept, breathed and shit the United States Army, and whenever he got the chance to screw over some short timer troop, especially a draftee, he was in hog heaven. This prick of a first sergeant didn't even wear the standard government issue jungle boots every troop received on arrival in Nam. He was beyond the fashion. Too good for them. Most of the time, when the brass were away at Long Binh he wore his regular stateside black military boots, spit shinned to a gleaming perfection by one of his "pet gooks."

Sergeant Bruno needed a back-alley tune-up. Many of us thought he ought to be fragged. With his chicken-shit attitude and asinine personality, he wouldn't have lasted a week in a jungle or a front line unit. The front liners would have sniped him and blamed it on the VC.

My good friend, Rory Robinson, the other bus driver (and a grand fellow), did his job to a fine tooth perfection, but with Bruno, was unfortunate as I was. He had

145

also received a speeding ticket while trying to dodge Viet Cong ammo, and was immediately bounced out of his job and replaced by a new recruit. Sergeant Bruno. . . oops, sorry, First Sergeant Bruno, shipped him out on his ass to Long Binh Army Depot before he could blink.

"Be careful of this bastard," Rory had told me. "The man gets his rocks off by screwing over anyone. Especially two-year draftees."

I dreaded this meeting. The first thing Bruno said when I walked into his office was, "Bowman, I see that an MP caught you speeding just this side of the Cong Paddie area."

"Yes, sir, first sergeant."

He began to go berserk. "Bowman," he bellowed, "Don't you call me sir ever again, got that? I actually work for a damned livin'! You don't see any damn bars or birds on my shoulders, do you?"

"No, I don't, first sergeant."

Then he said, "Bowman, do you like being in the United States Army?"

I said, "It's okay, first sergeant."

"You mean the army is just okay, right?"

This jackass lifer was having a ball. "First sergeant," I replied, "I didn't choose to enlist in the army. I took the draft."

"Well, you must not like the army very well if you chose the two year draft over enlisting."

"It wasn't necessarily a matter of liking the army or not. I had a real good job driving a fire truck and running a fire crew for the California Division of Forestry. First sergeant, would you allow me to explain my duties as a fire truck driver for the forestry?"

"I really don't know what this bullshit has to do with your speeding ticket," he said, cold as a fish, "But go ahead, spit it the hell out."

"Look, first sergeant," I started in, "I'm not trying to be funny here. I'm only trying to tell you my job duties as a fire truck driver for the most respected forestry fire protection agency in the United States."

He interrupted with, "Hurry the hell up. I don't have much time for this crap."

"As a fireman and a fire truck driver, I was called out on many emergency calls, such as forest fires, structure fires, vehicle fires and sometimes emergency medical aid. I usually had from two to four firefighters on the truck with me. I was a very reliable and a very conscientious fire truck driver."

"Did you use your red lights and siren when you went on your emergency runs?"

"Yes, I did, first sergeant, it's the California State vehicle law."

"You know what, Specialist Bowman," he shot back, "I think you like to drive real fast. Maybe you think that damned army bus you used to drive was a fire truck! By the way Specialist, I did say the bus you used to drive. Do you see any damned red lights or a screaming-ass siren on that bus you drive?"

"No," first sergeant," I answered, "I was only trying to. . . " (Clearly, he didn't want to hear about my reason for speeding.)

"Look here, I don't give a flying rat's-ass about your damned fire truck job in California."

I went ahead anyhow. "First Sergeant Bruno, my entire load of new recruits and I were in the middle of a big firefight battle with a couple of units or more of

NVA and Viet Cong, and I thought I was doing the right thing. I managed the bus through the whole ordeal without a scratch, except for a blown out rear tire. I was only doing what I thought at the time was safest and in the best interest for my busload of recruits and myself."

It got me nowhere. He didn't give a damn. "I don't really care what you think anymore, Bowman," he ranted, "Nor do I want any more of your bullshit. And I need to get back to work." Then, after a glance at the clock, he added, "I'm replacing you with a *competent* bus driver. When in processing selects a replacement for your position, I want you to show him the ropes. Teach him all the stops in Long Binh, and teach him everything you know about the job. Got that?"

I was steaming inside, but I said, "Yes, first sergeant."

He went on. "You're gonna be shipping out to a heavy duty truckin' company, and if you think the Charlies were dangerous out on the road between here and Long Binh, you'd better think again. This job I've selected is a real sweetheart son-of-a-bitch. You're gonna learn to obey and play by the U.S. Army rules, not yours. Got that, Bowman?"

I could feel the urge to strangle this sawed-off lifer bastard bubbling up inside. But I held my tongue. "Yes, first sergeant," I replied. Then, thinking fast but keeping my question brief and to the point so he wouldn't get pissed off again, I asked him if I personally located another job within our 1st Logistical Command, if that would be OK.

"I'll give you twenty-four hours," he shot back. "Exactly one full day to find something within our command. Then that's it, you're out of here. Got it?"

"Yes first sergeant," I said.

The man was a real piece of work. Twenty-four hours seemed impossible. And exceptionally unreasonable. But I had to give it a try, and I knew I'd have to work fast. As I left his office I decided that this stump of a sergeant had a major dose of the little man's syndrome, and to top it off, he must have been standing in the wrong line when they passed out the brains.

All shook up about having to ship out to some hellhole jungle unit, I recalled that my friend Rory had sent me a note a couple of months back. I'd stored it at my bunk area in the hooch, and in the note, as I remembered, he'd mentioned something about contacting him if I ever ran into trouble with First Sergeant Bruno.

I ran down to the hooch, got out my shoe box full of letters and cards, sorted through the pile and found Rory's. Towards the end of his letter Rory said, "I wouldn't put too much trust in that goddamned first sergeant or the company commander. Officer Hamilton should overrule that little son-of-a-b Bruno once in a while, but he's got no damned balls. That commander is nothing but a greenhorn, young punk lifer and a real wimp, filling a chair and nothing else. Ivan, if you run into trouble, it'll probably be from Bruno, not that weak-ass Hamilton. If you do, I might be able to help. I work for a full bird colonel over here, and he doesn't like some of the army bullshit that's been going on. You can reach me most of the time on the landline, at this number, 7755. Regardless, give me a call sometime and let me know how you're doing."

I called him early the next morning. "Rory," I said, "Bruno's shipping me out of here, like pronto, in just a few short days, to a jungle trucking unit. I'm scared half to death and if I don't do something fast, this is gonna happen! Can you do me any good? Are you in any kind of position to help me locate a job over there, within our command?"

"I make no promises," said Rory, "But call me back at 1500 hours sharp, that'll give me enough time to see what I can scrounge up."

I called Rory back at 1500 hours sharp. "Bowman," he said, "Your timing is perfect. I've located three job openings. If you want them, that is."

"Want them?! Like I've got a choice? I'll take almost anything over that jungle unit. What do ya have?"

"Well, I remembered that you'd told me you'd been a part time cook back in some Northern California forestry fire camp. So I happened to run down a mess hall cook's position. And another bus driver job. Plus a clerical position in a big motor pool, comparable to the battalion maintenance clerk job you had back at Fort Hood."

I told Rory the clerk job at the motor pool sounded great.

Though extremely relieved, I still had a major hurdle: I had to run the whole transfer thing by my belligerent first sergeant and the pussyfoot company commander. But if Bruno and Hamilton did approve the new clerk's position, I'd still be assigned within our same command. Just a change in duty and location to HHC, Headquarters and Headquarters Company, Saigon Support Command, Long Binh, 1st Logistical Command, Corps III.

With all the particulars about the motor pool clerk position obtained from Rory, and nervous as a fresh recruit ordered to charge across no-man's land after the enemy, I took a deep breath and stepped into my cocky first sergeant's office once again. I stood there, silent as death, while he scanned the particulars. Then he looked up and said, "You're a lucky bastard, Bowman, because I was having your transfer orders prepared tomorrow to have your ass shipped out of here in three days flat to a sweetheart, commie-infested jungle trucking unit. Do you realize how long you'd have lasted out there?"

"No, first sergeant," I replied, "I really have no way of knowing that. I'm not a God or a genius."

"I hope you're not getting smart with me," he said, glaring. Then he went on with, "I don't know whose ass you kissed to get this pansy motor pool job but you've lucked out. Somebody must be looking out for you, Bowman. If I had my way, I'd have you driving heavy trucks and humping for the ground pounders. Now get your tall, skinny-ass out of here before you are." And he pointed his stubby little finger at the door.

"Yes, first sergeant," I said, "Thank you for your time." I wasn't about to make any more waves. I didn't make a single peep, just turned around and left.

To finally get away from him was a blessing.

Some creative and talented troop with clever humor and tremendous artistic ability scrolled out a sketch of our truly despised Bruno on the shithouse walls. Unbelievable toilet talent! The industrious troop drew a cigar-smoking First Sergeant Bruno with his jungle fatigues down around his ankles sitting on the mighty throne taking a dump. On the white stall wall below were the words, "*Extra, extra, read all about it! The perfect soldier, First Sergeant Bruno, a lifer's dream. He eats Army, he shits Army. Army's biggest asshole, this roll's for you!*" An arrow pointed straight down to the toilet paper roll, and there was just as much smoke belching up from the throne as there was spewing out of his fat, short Havana stogie. A hilarious and most appropriate scene. Right on the money.

Sadly, this toilet humor was an accurate reflection of the blundering military mind and the many pompous, arrogant lifers who made up the army in Nam. Many of the so-called leaders we had to defer to – the brass,

151

junior officers and NCOs – were totally incompetent. Some were even disgracefully dishonest and downright absurd. Honorable conduct and integrity among many of the lifers towards the lower-ranking soldier was rare, especially in the rear echelon units.

Within three days, I received my orders to ship out to Long Binh. In the meantime, I trained the new bus driver replacing me. I took him through the entire route and the various unit stops at the big Long Binh base, until I felt reasonably sure that he had the job down pat. Then I left it up to him and started to prepare to ship out to my new motor pool job.

As I got on the bus for Long Binh, the same one I had ridden to the 537th PSC back in December of 1968, the same one I'd been in charge of and in which I'd transported so many new recruits, I was feeling severely hurt and let down by the United States Army. Along with several other newly arrived replacement recruits, I had been reduced to being merely a passenger. While it was a relief to be out of Bruno's jurisdiction, and while I admit to having done a lot of crazy things, when it came to troop transport reliability and quality performance, I could always be counted on. I knew that I was a conscientious and dedicated soldier.

What an odd feeling. It didn't seem right. I didn't deserve this crap. I hadn't been brought up to be a loser. The only thing I'd done was to try to save my recruits by racing through a major VC and NVA firefight. And what did I get for it? I had to deal with assholes like the brain-dead, trigger-happy MP. And Bruno too. Both of them making arbitrary and thoughtless decisions based on half backed evidence. So the army, I decided, was being disloyal and disrespectful to some of its most dedicated and patriotic soldiers. Not only did they betray some of their best, but they had also betrayed the army as a whole.

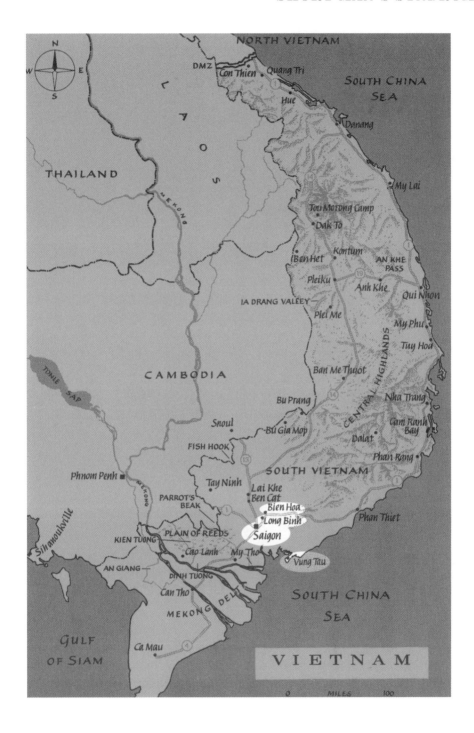

WHO'S MY ENEMY?

LAND OF ROUND-EYED GIRLS

NEW JOB, SAME OLD WAR.

Here I was again, the NG (new guy) at the motor pool in Long Binh Army Depot. A NG even though I was a seasoned soldier and had been in South Vietnam for several long, agonizing months. Soon after being introduced to all the brass and important NCOs, I was up to my ears in a ton of tedious and time-consuming paperwork.

Because of its insignia, a red circle with a bright blue interior and a white arrow placed in the center (but leaning slightly as if it was about to tip over), this command was dubbed "the leaning shit house." How appropriate.

To add to the load (pun intended), my lower intestinal tract was acting up again, worse than before, with constant diarrhea and puking. And I was losing one hell of a lot of weight and energy. When the agonizing discomfort became too much to bear, I headed back to the dispensary doctors for more tests. But they still couldn't figure out the problem. What in the hell was wrong with me?

The sicker I got, the more it seemed like the workdays dragged on and on, and the more the paperwork stacked up at the motor pool.

My job consisted of keeping current and accurate readiness reports, similar to what I'd been doing earlier with the 2nd Armored Division back at Fort Hood. The reports showed the status of all equipment housed at the motor pool and listed equipment that needed repair and parts in order to be combat ready. The situation was constantly changing, so it was important not to fall behind with the paperwork.

But with my insides doing the Texas Trot, something in my head clicked. I began thinking about R & R (rest and recreation). Maybe a long break would both relieve the monotony of the job and do some good for my gut. Just seeing some beautiful round-eyed girls in Australia, just the change of atmosphere, I thought, might give my ailing body a much-needed psychological boost. And who knows, maybe a physical one too. It wouldn't be that long before I was out of Nam, so if I could just hang on a little longer healthwise. . . Mulling the idea gave me something to look forward to, sort of the possibility of acquiring a new lease on life. So I put in a written request for R & R and within three weeks it was approved and I was on a 707, heading for the beautiful, round-eyed women of Sydney.

And just in case of an intestinal emergency, I conned the doctors into giving me a big dose of anti-diarrhea medicine. I almost laughed at the thought; there I'd be, making time with some lovely Aussie gal and suddenly my intestines go into a tailspin. Wouldn't that be the shits!

JUNE 1969. Normally, most married soldiers on R & R meet their ever lovin' wives in the great state of Hawaii, but the way I was feeling about Karen, I felt it would be a far better move to take mine "down under."

In spite of everything, I had a strong desire to see my beautiful wife, but my resentment over the adulteress affair I knew she was carrying on, plus her not writing, clearly meant she didn't give a damn. Well, what the hell; maybe there'd be some real fine action in Sydney. Maybe I'd hook up with some gorgeous Aussie. I'd had enough of Asian gals for a while. Don't get me wrong, there were some beautiful Vietnamese women, and many of the French-Vietnamese gals were stunning. But I still longed to feast my eyes on a bevy of round-eyed blond, brunet or redheaded beauties.

Sydney. By way of a greeting, our Aussie host gave our R & R troops a pleasant hospitality speech. She suggested we take brief notes on the best clothing stores, nightclubs, and most importantly, the best places to meet some fun-loving and good looking (and available, we hoped) Aussie women. We were more than attentive because we only had five days, so had to take full advantage of the time available. Especially when it came to locating the fair sex.

Many of the troops, including myself, went to a popular shop to rent dress suits and everything else that might help us cut a handsome figure. The Aussie ladies in the store were more than helpful in picking out the perfect attire. Then, all decked out and ready to live it up on my first evening in Sydney, I happened to meet two beautiful maids at the hotel where I was staying. Both these gals had great personalities, were friendly and pleasantly down to earth, and invited me to join them for a meal, prepared by one of their moms. How could I refuse? No way. And for two reasons: secretly licking my chops, I had fallen for their good looks – and I was hungry as a bear coming off a long winter's hibernation. After several long, agonizing months of army chow, home-cooked sounded perfect.

One of the gals, Barbara was a little overweight but had a pleasant disposition and a pretty face. The other, Marlena, looked like she'd just stepped out of a movie star magazine. She was a drop-dead gorgeous knockout.

Electrifying. She reminded me of the Australian singer and movie star, Olivia Newton-John.

We enjoyed a tasteful, old-fashioned dinner, at Barbara's home. The girls finished their meals in a hurry then excused themselves and skipped off into one of the bedrooms to get spruced up for a night on the town. As I quickly discovered, Aussie women don't beat around the bush when they decide to paint the town red. They're ready to go for the gusto. Full bore. I fell in love with their personalities and especially their Aussie accents and expressions, "mate this, mate that." Mate, mate, mate, and more mate. (And yes, I *did* hope to mate!)

I was stunned by how fast the girls dressed (to kill) with every essential: makeup, perfume, the works. I thanked Barbara's mother for a delightful dinner, then the girls and I headed for one of the many superb nightclubs in downtown Sydney.

Barbara seemed sweet on me, but my eyes couldn't stay off the strikingly beautiful Marlena. She was so easy to look at. Even though I couldn't help myself, I didn't want to hurt Barbara's feelings. So I went along with the program while awaiting the right opportunity. Like the Big Bad Wolf stalking Little Red Riding Hood.

When we sat down in the nightclub bar, Barbara leaned over and whispered, "Hey there mate, can you set up my friend, Marlena with a date for the evening? The night's still young, what d'ya think, mate?" For a moment, I was in a trance. Boy, oh boy, I thought, would I like to be her date. Then I came out of it. "Barb, let me think about that for a moment," I said. "If a soldier I know is still over at the hotel, I might be able to reach him." And all the time I'm thinking that the odds of my friend still being in his room were pretty damned slim. But wanting to do the decent thing, I decided to give it a try. I told Barb that I'd met this GI on the jet flying over from Nam. I called the hotel, sort of hoping my buddy wasn't there. But as luck would have it he was still screwing around in his room. And it was already 10:00 PM. Why, I never asked him, but every other R & R vet in Sydney was out and about by now, dancing, drinking and having a ball.

To make a long story short, I told my GI friend that I had a knockout of a blind date for him and he needed to get his sleepy-ass over to this nightclub before somebody beat him to it.

"Okay, Bowman," he said, "But I'll bet she's some kind of lard-can Aussie gal that can't find a date, and I'm gonna be the sucker."

I said, "You goofy bastard, just get your butt out of that hotel and find out for yourself."

This guy's gonna flip out when he sees Marlena, I thought. I can't believe I'm letting this beauty slip through my fingers.

In the meantime, as we sat at the bar sipping cocktails, Barbara who had begun to sense that I was down in the dumps, looked at me closely and said, "Lynn, I think you sort of like my friend, here, Marlena." Trying to hide my true feelings, I said, "No way, no, no, no." Though of course I did have the hots for Marlena. She was so refreshingly beautiful that I could taste her.

"Listen here, mate," said Barbara, "I know you like her better than you like me. You can't fool me on this one. She's so darn attractive, you know it and I know it, and I really can't blame you for being fascinated with her." Then she got kind of huffy and said, "I kind of wanted to have a good time with you tonight, but I've noticed your undivided attention toward Marlena, so I can see my good times are washed down the damn drain. The night is shot for me, so mate I'm gonna make a real scene or something." Before I could even get in a word she shouted, "Go to hell you son-of-a-bitch!" And with that she picked up her cocktail, splashed it in my face and abruptly stormed off.

I wanted to put my head in a hole. Everyone at the bar was staring at me, wondering what I'd done to piss-off the nice young Aussie lady. I must have been some dirty bastard, is what their looks said. The beauty queen Marlena, however, just sat there on her bar stool a few seats over, without a word, and wondering, what in the hell was going on with her best friend. Somewhat to my surprise, she didn't move an inch or get up and go after Barbara. Puzzling. For my part, I didn't know what to say or do, so I kept my mouth shut and sat quietly, allowing the cocktail to evaporate on my face and on my nice, rented dress suit.

Off in the midst of the crowded nightclub, a tall, good-looking blonde was singing. I kept sitting there, sipping my cocktail, watching her, and all the time thinking how desperately I wanted to make a move on sweet Marlena. But I didn't have the guts. Because I'd set up my GI friend from the hotel with her as a blind date, and also because I thought she might get ticked-off if she found out that I'd sort of dumped on her best friend. So I reluctantly decided to just wait for my friend, and then I'd be free to start shopping around.

An hour later my buddy finally showed up. "It's about goddamn time," I said. I'd committed myself to get him this date, so I couldn't back out now.

My friend, Tom, asked, "Where's my date, Bowman? Are you playing some kind of April fools joke, or what?"

"No joke at all," I replied, "And it's June, not April. Your date is right over there," I said, indicating Marlena, sitting on the tall bar stool and tending her cocktail.

Tom looked toward her for several moments, then turned back to me and said, annoyed, "Come on Bowman, you're playin' a trick on me, lets get real here, stop jacking me around."

"I've told you once, and now I've told you twice, numb-nuts, its no joke, that's your date!"

Tom said, "Really?"

"Really."

"But she's so absolutely stunning, it scares me half to death. She looks like she could be in the movies, she's beyond my wildest dreams, Bowman. I don't rate that good."

I said again, "That's your date, stupid-ass, you better get over there and get with the program and introduce yourself. Or would you like me to introduce you?"

"No, I'll take charge," he said, "But Bowman, I'm trembling in my shoes, I hope I can make a good impression and not trip over my own tongue."

"Holy cow, you dumb schmuck, can't you handle a little beauty? Think of it this way – she's only looking for companionship, so get your butt over there like a man, and if you can't handle that I'll be damn glad to step in for you."

Every since I had met Marlena, I couldn't keep my eyes off her. The chick captivated me. I'd have crawled through twenty miles of ground glass and tiger shit just to shake the man's hand that manufactured her douche bag.

Well, scardy-cat Tom finally got up enough guts and introduced himself, and right away, to my great surprise (and vast displeasure) it seemed like they hit it off pretty well. So there I sat, sad, sulking and screwed. My friend with Marlena, and me left with nothing but a drink in my hand as I tried to focus on the tall, attractive blonde who stood by the grand piano, singing.

A few moments later, I started chatting with another troop. There we were, two good-looking GI Joes, still dateless at 11 p.m. and just sitting there bullshitting when we knew we'd much rather be wining, dining and dancing with some beautiful Aussie gals. Still, it was a hell of a lot better than being in Vietnam, dealing with ass-wipe lifers and dodging the Charlies.

All at once, someone on the bar stool that had previously been occupied by chubby Barbara, bumped my arm. I turned, and to my surprised astonishment it was the tall, good-looking blonde singer I'd been watching off and on for the past couple hours.

"Pardon me mate," she said, "Sorry that I bumped you. Hope I didn't disturb you."

You can bump me any old time, I thought to myself. Then, unbelievably, she asked, "Would you like a drink, mate?"

Dumbfounded is not the word. I couldn't believe my ears. "Absolutely," I replied, smiling. During the first cocktails (which she bought), we introduced ourselves. Her name was Vivian. We talked, danced, had a few more cocktails and had a terrific time.

Later, we caught a trolley car, a major mode of transportation in Sydney. Vivian told the conductor she wanted to go to a certain part of the city, apparently, near her home. The conductor, a gruff old bearded character, replied in a sharp, deep grumble, "You damn well know Missy this train car doesn't go out there at this time of night." Then he eyed her quizzically and asked, "You all right Missy, have you had too damn much to drink?"

Vivian didn't exactly know what to say. It seemed as if she wanted both me and the conductor to think she was prim and proper, and not up to any hanky-panky. But I had a strong hunch she had another agenda. The conductor caught on and winked at me.

I asked him to head for my hotel. And since Vivian didn't say a word, she apparently had no objection.

We were still pretty tipsy from all the cocktails when we got there, and we staggered a bit and laughed going up the stairs. As we approached the door to my room Vivian whispered in my ear, "Listen here, Lynn, I'm just coming in for a brief visit, nothing else."

"Sure, Vivian, that's fine with me."

We weren't in the room thirty seconds before all our clothes were off and on the floor. And I don't have to tell you the rest of the story.

The next morning, I awoke to a profusion of beautifully natural blonde hair on the pillow next to me. I was stunned. Twenty-four hours before I'd been in the war-torn land of Vietnam, and today I was waking up next to a charming, blue-eyed blonde. That's what life is all about, I suppose: change. Suddenly, everything was fantastic and wonderfully worthwhile. I felt alive again.

We spent all five days of my R & R together. The closer we became, the more Vivian loosened up and confided in me, relating stories of her hard life as the daughter of an Auckland, New Zealand commercial fisherman, about meeting another fisherman whose charming manner disarmed her. And how, after luring her below deck in his fishing boat, he immediately demanded sex. Then, after a furious verbal and physical battle, how he'd gone nearly berserk and, with a knife at her throat, finally forced her to submit. Because of the distinct possibility that her father would have searched out and most likely killed the deranged sexual pervert, she had never told him. And after the local police – who she figured were buddy-buddy with the fishing community – did absolutely nothing, she'd decided to split from her horrible memories in Auckland and cross the Tasmanian Sea for Sydney, where she eventually became a successful singer. Vivian had whispered not a word of this to her father, fearing he might become unglued, and, with his violent temper, probably kill the man who had disgraced his only daughter.

Her story touched me deeply, and that, combined with who she was as a person, convinced me I was in love.

During our five days, Vivian guided me through the beautiful city and introduced me to many of her friends and coworkers. I quickly came to the conclusion that I'd never seen so many beautiful women in one place in my entire life. One evening while Vivian and I were hanging out at the Australian Hotel, a very popular place for Aussie girls to meet soldiers, we danced to a live band, met friends, and enjoyed several strong cocktails. That night was particularly memorable because there must have been half a dozen gals to every GI in the place. If at any time a man ever wanted to try for two of these Aussie beauties, this would've been the time and the place. Of course, I don't know what a guy would do with two of these energetic gals, because I had my hands completely full with one. But it was an interesting thought.

My five days were up too fast. It wasn't fair. If anyone could fall in love in five days, I was sure I'd done it. But now I had to say goodbye. When I got up that last morning and dressed in my civvies, Vivian lay there still asleep. Tears began to trickle down my face as I stood looking at this beautiful woman that I'd never see again. We had had such wonderful fun together, it was beyond words. And now it was over. I had to return to a world of dumb-ass idiot army lifers, firefights and body bags.

I was completely dressed now. I bent over, gently brushed her hair aside and kissed her on the forehead. She awoke, and we hugged and embraced for a short moment. I began to cry again as I mumbled, "I love you sweetheart, I love you, I have to go, and I'm late!" Teary-eyed, I walked to the door. I turned back for one last look. She was sitting up in bed, tears streaming down her lovely face. We were both completely heartbroken. I threw her a kiss and walked out the door.

I boarded the airport bus and chose a seat on the hotel side. GIs were boarding from all over. Most, I was sure, were dreading the trip back to Nam as much as I was. As I sat there in the bus in sort of a mental stupor I happened to look out, and there on the sidewalk in front of the hotel were the two Aussie gals I'd first met, chubby Barbara and her beauty queen friend, Marlena. Apparently, they were seeing some GIs off and saying their goodbyes. For a moment I thought about shouting goodbye, but I really wasn't in too good a mood, so I just sat watching the troops climb aboard. And thinking of the sweetheart I'd left with tears streaming down her face back in the hotel room.

Behind me, a GI was hanging out the bus window, holding hands with a sad, heart-struck Aussie girl as she wept like a baby, begging her lover-boy to stay and go AWOL. And there's weren't the only Aussie and GI hearts left broken. It happened to hundreds. But even though I had loved, in a way I didn't feel like I'd lost. Better to have what Vivian and I had than never to have loved at all.

A dimwitted Aussie soldier sitting in the bus finally had too much of the sobbing from the brokenhearted Australian girl clinging tightly to the GI. He leaned out his window and in a full blown Aussie accent said, "Hey little gal, don't cry, don't cry, it won't be long and another bloody busload of high grade USDA meat will be arriving soon. So wipe your tears, Missy, and put a big smile back on that face and get ready for the next load of choice tube steaks!"

These Australian troops were a hard-core bunch, and their sense of humor got a little raw at times. But I guess I could understand their resentment.

The band was pretty good and the place was filled with some really nice roundeyed girls. But unfortunately it was also filled with a lot of Yanks on R&R so we didn't have a chance with the girls. The band was only playing American songs and as the drinks went down our anger went up. They started playing the Yellow Rose of Texas. . . that was the last straw. F**k it, we had gone away to fight a war no one liked, we were ignored when we came back, or jeered. . . and now in our own country we couldn't even talk to an Aussie girl or listen to our own music. Someone (I don't know who) walked up to the band and requested Waltzing Matilda . . . the band laughed at him. . . he was told to sit down and shut up. He returned to the table and relayed the conversation. We left the table and shut and barricaded the bar doors.

All went quiet. . . the patrons were informed that we had just returned from the 'Nam and that we wanted to hear something Australian and that if we didn't then this bar was in serious danger of being torn apart. The band played Waltzing Matilda. . . and then we left. We said goodbye on the streets of the Cross - with the prostitutes, pimps, drunks and junkies as our witnesses.

<small>AN AUSTRALIAN SOLDIER'S MEMORY OF RETURNING HOME FROM VIETNAM.[1]</small>

---

[1]Fifty thousand Australians served in Vietnam. Five hundrd were killed.

Over hill, over dale, as we hit the dusty trail

As the lifers go stumbling along,

Watch them drink, watch them stink,

Watch them even try to think,

As the lifers go stumbling along.

For it's heigh heigh hee, truly fucked are we,

Shout out your numbers loud and strong. R.A.!

For where e're you go, you will always know

That the lifers go stumbling along.

Stumble! Stumble! Stumble!

VIETNAM DRAFTEE PARODY, SUNG TO THE TUNE OF

"THE CAISSONS GO ROLLING ALONG"

TOAST TO JACK DANIELS

I get by with a little help from my friends.

John Lennon

THE R & R, AND ESPECIALLY THE LOVELY VIVIAN, had done my body a world of good. My gut problems had subsided somewhat, my general health had improved, and that felt great. Until I returned to my desk, that is. A mountain of paperwork awaited me and it took days to catch up.

Right away, my insides began doing somersaults again. So back to the dispensary for more damned tests and examinations. The continual worry about my chronic diarrhea, vomiting, itching rashes, and weight loss gradually took its toll. Was I headed for a hospital? Worse? For a while, I wondered if I'd get out of Nam alive.

When I'd arrived back in December 1968, I'd weighed 210 pounds. In July, 1969, I was down to 188. That may not sound terrible, but I'm over six-foot three, and at the rate I was going, what could I expect to weigh in three to four more months?

I wanted to get out of this mind-shattering hellhole of Vietnam so damned bad. But couldn't bear the thought that I might have to be carried out because of some stupid, idiotic disease. It just didn't sound military. And certainly not honorable. I wanted to serve my comrades

169

(if not the United States Army) until my time was up, and depart the war with dignity. And no, I damn sure wasn't hoping to get wounded, or come home with a medal pinned to my chest inside one of those depressing silver-aluminum morgue boxes!

Of course, no soldier knew what his final destiny would be in Vietnam. But I was definite about one thing: I wanted to try to salvage what life I had left and make it count for something. The only chance I had, I figured, was to try to forget the self-pity and hang on healthwise.

The doctors had no idea what to do about my deteriorating condition. I'm not saying that they didn't care, or try (unless they were just going through the motions). It was simply that nothing they suggested seemed to be working

One sweltering evening, while visiting with my good friend Specialist Rory Robinson, I brought up the subject of my deteriorating health. Rory had been helpful before, so I thought he might have a suggestion. "Why not put in for an early-out?" he said. "If it gets approved, that would knock maybe ninety full days off your tour."

Ninety days less! Boy, oh boy, that sounded like a gift from heaven. I jumped on Rory's suggestion and wrote home to my parents, telling them about the early-out possibility. "Contact my old boss, Ranger Dave German at the California Division of Forestry's Sutter Hill Fire Station." I asked them, "And please ask him to write a brief letter requesting that I be released from active duty in Vietnam to return to my permanent job, fighting forest fires and driving forest-fire trucks. And make sure he convinces the army that because of the extreme fire danger during the summer of 1969, my experience as a seasoned fireman is essential."

I sure hoped a letter from German would do it.

It didn't take long for a reply. About mid July I received the requested letter and submitted it to my commanding officer; with some concern, because Ranger German kind of screwed up in the letter's last sentence. "Mr. Ivan Bowman," it said, "Will be reinstated to his permanent fire-truck driving position regardless of when he's released from the war in Vietnam."

Which meant they could keep me here until my scheduled tour was complete. But I had no choice, I had to submit the letter. It went through the proper channels of military BS, along with my personal request for a ninety-day release from active duty. But I was flat-ass turned down. Which meant they could keep me until the cows came home, or until my scheduled tour of duty was complete.

Disappointed? To say the least. German's last sentence had spelled my doom. The information that I could have my old job back "regardless of when he's released. . . " smothered my hopes. Just like putting out the small fire of hope that was kindling inside me.

Well, if at first you don't succeed, try, try again and all that. . . So I went back down to the orders office, where I happened to run into the specialist who was head clerk for orders and leaves. Very similar in knowledge and ability to my good friend Fred Freeman back at my old unit at Fort Hood, this fellow was wonderfully congenial. So I told him about the situation and asked if there was any way he could resubmit the request.

"I can run it back through my commander's office," he replied, "But don't get your hopes up, you may not have any more luck than with your first submission." Then he asked, "How come you want this early-out so damned bad?"

I told him about my health problems and elaborated on my concern about what might happen if I didn't get competent medical help. He seemed concerned, so I continued babbling on. I was about to say something about my wife cheating on me while I was stuck in this Godforsaken war, but then thought he might wonder why I'd want to go home to an unfaithful wife. So I dropped that idea like a hot rock. I did, however, mention that I was married and had a baby girl that I couldn't wait to see. Maybe, I thought, that would be the clincher.

The clerk nodded then asked, "Is it true that they have some pretty bad forest fires out there in the hills and mountains of California?"

"Damn straight," I said. "The worst generally hit in late July, August and September, and sometimes the fire season will push into October and beyond. Especially if we've had a real hot, dry and windy season. And sometimes those fierce, fall Santa Ana winds fan the flames and raise havoc with everyone and everything – including the firemen!"

The clerk looked at me hard. "Bowman," he said, "You really do look sort of thin. Your face is drawn and your color doesn't look quite right. Maybe you *should* try and get the hell out of here. I'll resubmit your request tomorrow morning."

I spent the next week with my fingers and toes crossed. Then, standing in the mail line one day I heard, "Hey, Bowman, Bowman, over here. . . Right here." It was the orders clerk. I instantly broke out of line and ran over to him.

"Bowman," he said, smiling, "You're out of here, you lucky bugger."

This was the best news I'd ever heard. "Are you sure?," I asked. "You're not jivin' me?"

"You're just as good as gone, guaranteed."

Good as gone, he'd said. Guaranteed! I was thrilled beyond words. Then the clerk said, "Come over to my office and I'll give you the approved orders."

"How the hell did you do it?," I asked. "What did you tell your commander when you resubmitted?"

He laughed, then said, confidentially, "Knowing that a second attempt would probably be denied, I deliberately hand carried it into his office so that I could personally explain your circumstances. I told him you were a friend and about your chronic intestinal disorders and being needed to fight forest fires in California and all the other bullshit. I kind of know how he operates and over time, I've learned from my job what it takes to get the hell out of Nam."

I stood there listening, amazed.

The clerk continued. "For a minute he had me worried, because he remembered that he'd denied the same request a few days before. But I guess he also remembered he owed me a favor."

"I'll be down to your office to pick up the orders before something goes wrong," I said, "And the officer changes his mind."

The clerk laughed and said, "I doubt that'll happen."

I said, "What can I do for ya, buddy? I really appreciate what you've done. How's about my next month's GI check?"

"No way," he replied, waving me off. "Nothing like that. Just get me a big-ass bottle of Jack Daniels."

"That sure sounds appropriate, but is that all?"

"Bowman," he replied, "It's all in the line of duty!"

"You're one hell of a good man," I said, slapping him on the back. "I'm gonna take care of you." I headed straight to the PX, picked up two big bottles of Jack Daniels and carried them in a bag directly into his office and set them on his desk. "I'll make you a deal," I said, "I'll trade you two bottles of Jack Daniels for one set of early-out orders. Does that sound like a fair deal?"

"Sounds fair enough to me, Bowman," he replied.

We made the trade and shook hands. I said, "Thanks a million, pal, you don't know what you've done for me. Keep the faith. And keep your head down!"

Specialist Rory Robinson had made the suggestion that led directly to my early out. I was going home in less than a week, and I had to share the good news with him first. So I decided to surprise him with a round of drinks.

When we met, I told him about the clerk and the two bottles of Jack Daniels that were my passport out of Nam. Before I'd said another word, Rory asked if I'd been absent much from my motor pool job because of my intestinal problems. Why was he asking that, I wondered.

"I've never really kept track of the time I took off for sick call," I replied, "But I'm damn sure of one thing; it was only time off for health problems, I wasn't out goofing off." Then I thought for a moment and added, "I did take off time for R & R, but came back to a shitload of paperwork. I was swamped for a few days until I caught up."

Rory said, "I'm gonna tell ya something very important, and listen real good on this one. Only notify your commanding officer in the motor pool three days prior to shipping out. That's the golden rule, because if you tell those damned lifer sons-a-bitches right away, they're gonna give ya all kinds of extra duties and anything else they can dig up."

"Won't they get all pissed-off and I'll get into all kinds of trouble?" I asked.

"Sure they'll be pissed off, but the dirty bastards can't touch you. Like I said, just notify them no more than three days before you head for your final out-processing."

"Are you absolutely sure on this?"

"I guarantee it. You'll be fine."

I smiled. Then I produced the other bottle of Jack Daniels I'd bought and we poured ourselves a whiskey and Coke and clanked our cups together.

"Bowman," said Rory, "Do you know that ever since that bastard short-ass peckerhead, First Sergeant Bruno, shipped me out of my bus driver job at the 537th for speeding away from a bunch of Charlies, I've been pissed-off. And then he did the same damn thing to you. What a lot of uncalled for army bullshit."

I said, "Remember the old saying? There's the right way, the wrong way and the army way? Well there's one they forgot: the lifer's stupid way."

We both cracked up on that, then Rory said, "Pour me another drink, Bowman. Even thinking about these lifers drives me to drink. Anyway, we're not gonna change one goddamned thing in this man's army, nor the lifers in it. You couldn't pay me a million bucks to re-up in this shit-hole outfit."

"Yeah the military isn't for me either."

"You know, Bowman, the other day my commanding officer asked me if I'd consider staying in the army and making a career of it? I just shook my head and said, 'Sir, no disrespect, you're one of the best career men I've ever been associated with, but I can't say that for most of the other career commissioned officers and NCOs.' And you know what? My full bird commander reached out and shook my hand, and said, 'I have to agree with you Rory, you've got too much upstairs to waste twenty years of your life. The United States Army used to be an honorable outfit, but no more. I've got fifteen more months myself, and I'll have my twenty years in. And then I'm out. And damned glad I'll be done with it.' "

I shook my head then said, "Let's forget about the United States Army and all the crap, because this may be our last chance to tip a couple. Lets have one more of these, they taste pretty damned good on a hot night, don't they? And before I forget, I want to give you my home address back in the world, so you can drop me a line and let me know how you're doing with the lifers and the Charlies."

"Sounds good to me," he said, "Pour me another strong dose of whisky, that's damn fine stuff!" I did; and secretly toasted to Jack Daniels, my one-way ticket home.

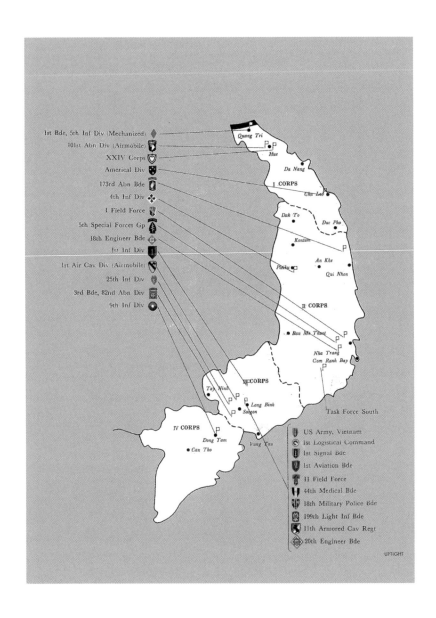

1st Bde, 5th Inf Div (Mechanized)
101st Abn Div (Airmobile)
XXIV Corps
Americal Div
173rd Abn Bde
4th Inf Div
I Field Force
5th Special Forces Gp
18th Engineer Bde
1st Inf Div
1st Air Cav Div (Airmobile)
25th Inf Div
3rd Bde, 82nd Abn Div
9th Inf Div

Quang Tri
Hue
Da Nang
I CORPS
Chu Lai
Duk To
Duc Pho
Kontum
An Khe
Pleiku
Qui Nhon
II CORPS
Ban Me Thuot
Nha Trang
Cam Ranh Bay
III CORPS
Tay Ninh
Long Binh
Saigon
Task Force South
IV CORPS
Dong Tam
Vung Tau
Can Tho

US Army, Vietnam
1st Logistical Command
1st Signal Bde
1st Aviation Bde
II Field Force
44th Medical Bde
18th Military Police Bde
199th Light Inf Bde
11th Armored Cav Regt
20th Engineer Bde

UPTIGHT

178

FOUR DAYS AND COUNTING

Historically "draftees" have kept the military on the straight and narrow. By calling a spade a spade, they keep it clean. Without their "careers" to think about, they can't be as easily bullied or intimidated as Regulars; their presence prevents the elitism that otherwise might allow a Regular army to become isolated from the values of the country it serves. Draftees are not concerned for the reputation of their employer, the Army (in Vietnam they happily blew the whistle on everything from phony valor awards to the secret bombings of Laos and Cambodia); a draftee, citizen's army, so much a part of the history of America, is an essential part of a healthy democracy, one in which everyone pays the price of admission.

COLONEL DAVID H. HACKWORTH (U.S. ARMY, RETIRED)

THE CLOCK WAS TICKING. Time was getting real *short*. (That's the term we used.) Four days to go before the big freedom bird would lift me out of Vietnam. This would certainly be alarming news to my commander, Officer Greene at the motor pool, when I approached him three days before I was due to leave. Like most lifers, I thought he'd probably come unglued. He was aware that my discharge date was October 31, not August 1, and I expected the worst.

On the morning of the fourth day before leaving, I showed up at the motor pool and carried on with my normal routine, turning out regular maintenance

179

reports and other paperwork. Just to be reassured about the three-day rule that Specialist Robinson had told me about, I did a small investigation of my own, checking with some of the seasoned office clerks. They all pretty much agreed with Rory that though it was an "under the carpet" secret, army regulations said that I absolutely need not notify the brass any sooner. They also told me that on the third day before my discharge date it was mandatory that I start my final out-processing. Then, Officer Greene would have no choice but to release me so I'd have time to get everything done. While the brass gets all wound-up and pissed-off, moaning and groaning at the late inform notice, the clerks assured me there was not a damn thing they could legally do about it.

I sure hoped they were right. If they weren't I'd be dead meat and hung out to dry. But I decided to put my faith in Rory and the clerks and go for the gamble. I worked late that day, snuffing up all the paperwork, so that the lifers wouldn't have too many excuses to jump down my throat when I dropped them the bombshell. By the end of the day everything was in tiptop shape.

On the morning of day number three I walked into the motor pool office with my early-out shipping orders in hand. But, cleverly, I thought, I'd semi concealed them among a sheaf of maintenance reports. Officer Greene seemed to be in a heated argument with one of the NCOs, so I twiddled my thumbs and screwed around at my desk, waiting for the right moment. Which was no easy task, since I was in such a sweat.

An hour or so later everything had cooled down and the office was back to normal. Now was the moment. I knew I had to get it over with. My heart was racing so fast it felt like I'd run up Mount Everest.

"Good morning sir," I said, cheery.

"What's so good about it, Bowman? And what the hell are those papers in your hand?"

Here goes, I thought, the shit's gonna hit the fan. "Sir," I replied, "These papers are orders for me to ship out. It's an early-out, a ninety-day reduction from my normal tour of active duty in Vietnam, sir."

He was ready to bust a gut; eyes glaring, red face and all. And I hadn't even given him the worst news, about it all happening in three days.

"Bowman," he shouted, "How damn long have you known about this? That you were going to ship out?"

Almost holding my breath, I replied, "Well, sir, I think it's been about two weeks now."

"Bowman, let me know if I heard you correctly. If you knew about this early-out at least two weeks ago, why in the goddamned hell didn't you tell me sooner?"

"I. . . Uh, I didn't think of it, sir. I guess it just slipped my mind or something."

"It slipped your brainless mind, huh? Are you completely nuts? Let me fully understand this. . . when are you shipping out of Vietnam? Give me a straight goddamned answer, you dumb-ass-bastard, how many more days from now?"

"Sir, I'm shippin' out for the world in three days."

Officer Greene jumped up from his plush, kickback chair, the purple rising in his face. "Bowman, you son-of-a-bitch," he shouted, "Stand at attention when you're talking to me, you specialist punk!" He went completely berserk, shaking, and screaming at the top of his lungs with all this vehemence emanating from his sickening dog-breath mouth. Almost slobbering in my face, and practically foaming at the mouth, he yelled at the top of his lungs, "You're goin' home in three goddamned days, is that what I heard you say, you specialist no-account bastard?"

"Yes sir, that's right, sir."

"Bowman, why, why, why, didn't you tell me about this ten days ago, you damned, horse's ass?"

"Like I said before, sir, it sort of slipped my mind. But on the other hand, I really didn't think I had to."

"You say you didn't think you had to tell me, you wise-ass? Are you getting smart with an officer, Bowman?"

"No, sir, not at all, sir!"

Now my patience was running thin. I had tried to keep calm, but now I was as pissed off as this idiot lifer, and my temper was about to blow. But I also knew that if I let loose I'd take the sucker's head off. Fortunately, something deep inside me said, "Cool down, Ivan, this isn't the moment in the game to let yourself get in trouble." While I don't appreciate anyone screaming vulgar obscenities, and practically spitting in my face with their putrid breath, I figured I'd better hold my tongue and my temper.

Officer Greene continued to rant and rave, adding, "If I had it my way I'd completely screw up your chickenshit, early-out. But at this late date it's clearly out of my hands. Bowman, this is a direct order: get down to your damned desk and finish up the rest of your paper work before you ship out."

"Sir, no disrespect," I said, "But I actually am all caught up. I worked very late yesterday afternoon finishing up. So, pardon me sir, but I can't really stay much longer, I was told that I need to start my formal out-processing today."

He stood there glaring at me for one long moment then said, "Get the hell out of my sight, Bowman. You've got a lot of nerve coming in here and telling me this, you've really got me pissed off, and now I've got to find a replacement that's worth a shit for your clerk's position. Get the hell out of here! And by the way, I'm not done with you yet, Bowman. You'll see!"

I wondered what he meant by that last remark, but I didn't want to rile him any further, so I saluted, turned on my heel and walked out.

D-day (departure day) minus two. I'd received my final shipping orders. Everything seemed set. Except for one thing: Officer Greene (the prick) had canceled my good conduct medal for my tour of duty. This really got to me. So I immediately went back to the motor pool office and requested to see the lifer son-of-a-bitch.

"What can I do for you, Bowman?" growled Officer Greene, "I thought you'd be busy with your final out-processing."

"Sir," I replied, "That's exactly what I've been doing. But I've noticed a little problem with my final shippin' orders; I happened to notice that you, sir, denied my good conduct medal. May I ask you why you made that decision?"

"I really don't need any reason," Bowman, "Because I'm the goddamn head honcho around here, got that?"

"Sir, I'm serious about this. I asked a simple question and I really do think I deserve some kind of answer or explanation."

"Bowman," he shot back, "You're a subordinate lower-ranking specialist who means absolutely nothing to me. And besides, I don't need to give you any kind of explanation, got that? I'm your superior officer, you damn disrespectful troop. And if this conversation doesn't stop immediately, I might just give you an Article 15. You are excused, Bowman, get out of this office, you don't belong here any more."

"Yes, sir," I said, saluting, "I guess that's an order for me to leave." I turned and departed, steaming mad. There was no honorable reason for his not being willing to answer a simple question. My work performance had been excellent and I'd done an impeccable job as head clerk in the motor pool, so the only reason he had was because of his stupid-ass injured pride that I hadn't notified him soon enough about my early-out orders. That really stunk. And another reason, I figured, was that he wasn't going home – and I was.

Day number two also took me back to my old unit, the 537th Personnel Service Company, at Bien Hoa Army Base, for my final out-processing. I made the rounds and said my goodbyes to several good friends, including my old commanding officer, Captain Perry. We reminisced a bit and wished one another the best of luck.

Still fuming over this, I also showed one of my old acquaintances, Specialist Scully, where my good conduct medal had been removed in my final shipping orders. He shuffled through the paperwork, gandering for the denial. I could tell he was a competent clerk and knew by the rapid manner in which he flipped through the file, that he knew the regulations backwards and forwards.

"This denial is complete military bullshit," he said, "And without substantial evidence to back it up, it's basically illegal. Or at least seriously out of normal procedure."

He searched for a note, a letter or other relevant information. When he couldn't find anything he said, "Bowman, if you choose to, you could have the bastard written up for such an idiotic and dishonorable action." When I told him I'd sure like to do something about it, he brought the matter to the attention of his commanding officer and gave him a full explanation. The major in charge of the office overruled Officer Greene and granted me back the medal that I'd earned honorably in the first place.

Before taking off I asked, "Scully, how're the Charlies been treating you guys over here at the 537th PSC?"

"Well," he replied, "Not too damn bad. We've had a few RPGs, rockets, and a few mortars thrown our way but nothing real serious."

After we had chatted a bit more about my ridiculous motor pool lifer, Scully said, "You know, that guy needs his ass reamed out. I could screw up his records so bad that he'd learn never to mess with the regular troops again . . . if you follow my meaning." Then, with a sly smile, he added, "You know, I might even torch his damn records."

"Yeah? Good idea," I said, "But I really don't need any trouble right now, wouldn't want to get caught up in something like that."

He laughed, then said, "Bowman, by the time I take care of him you'll be trout fishin' up in the high Sierra streams. Just give me the thumbs up right now, or give me a call on the landline before you leave the Nam, and I'll really enjoy tightening the screws on that lifer bastard."

"I'd better think this one over," I said. "I'll let you know. And thanks for your tremendous help on my records. I appreciate your getting this good conduct medal fiasco straighted out. I've really got to go finish the rest of my out-processing now, but if I change my mind about Greene's records I'll let you know real soon. See ya, Scully." And I was off. I'm sure that Scully was serious about destroying Officer Greene's records; he had the crazy personality and it's obvious he had the know how. But I'd already decided not to risk any more difficulty, so I let the whole thing drop.

After leaving Scully I went back to my old hooch, where I discovered that Wino had served out his tour and left. I didn't find Frenchie, he was still on duty call. Just as well, I owed him an old gambling dept.

The last thing I needed to do was get special paperwork taken care of for my war-collected SKS Chinese communist rifle, the one I'd picked up off the dead Viet Cong on my AWOL trip with Frenchie to the whorehouse in the city of Bien Hoa.[2] During normal out-processing prior to their departure, military personnel could obtain clearance and transport papers for such Chinese or Russian made war keepsakes. Though by no means could we legally possess or transport any U.S. Government issued weapons back to the world.

When asked where, when and how I had acquired the enemy rifle I replied, "I found it near a dead Viet Cong, back in April, in the area of Cong Paddies, after a firefight located just off the main road between Long Binh and Bien Hoa Army Bases." (Well, two out of three answers were correct. That seemed fair enough. I actually did find the rifle near a dead VC, and the month was April 1969. If the lifer couldn't take a little April fool's joke, that was his problem.)

I could hardly wait. Tomorrow I'd be aboard a freedom bird, winging home.

[2] Captured SKS Chinese communist rifle. Serial Number 11389051

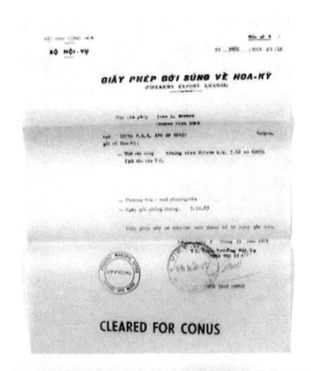

CLEARED FOR CONUS

VIETNAM VETERANS BOARD A HOMEWARD BOUND JETLINER

BACK TO THE WORLD

So it's home again, and home again,

America for me.

My heart is turning home again, and

there I long to be. . .

I want a ship that's westward bound to

plough the rolling sea

To the blessed Land of Room Enough

beyond the ocean bars,

Where the air is full of sunlight and the

flag is full of stars.

HENRY VAN DYKE, POET

FEW AMERICAN TROOPS regarded Vietnam as part of the civilized world. That was the good old U S of A. Nam always seemed like some kind of bad dream that we couldn't wait to wake up from.

August 1, 1969. D-Day. My last full day in Vietnam was coming to an end.

Discharge day, of course, was not necessarily a GIs' *final* discharge day, just his departure day. But in Vietnam it was the day he longed for, the day he cherished, the day he would catch a flight back to the world on a freedom bird. For most draftees their final ETS, (end, or expired term of service) would follow as soon as they arrived back in the States. If you were an enlisted man or a career soldier, your final ETS might not arrive until a few short months or even several years later, depending on your time left to serve.

Now I just had to wait patiently at the huge personnel-shipping depot at Long Binh Army Base and listen for the announcement for the bus to Bien Hoa Airfield, the place I'd been to so many times before while driving the bus for the 537th PSC. But now, it was my time in the spotlight, my turn to fly home.

Every troop with orders to ship out waited in one of several large barracks. I chose a fairly empty one, way in the back forty, since I was a bit concerned that my old buddy Frenchie might have heard the scuttlebutt from my old GI friends at Bien Hoa Army Base that I was shipping out and he'd come searching me out to claim an old gambling debt. I'd played and lost several hard fought card games in a row. Cribbage. Each time I had doubled the damn bet, hoping to win the next game. But with my dumb luck, I got skunked. I'd told Frenchie that I'd pay the debt as soon as I got my hands on enough money, but it never happened. To be perfectly honest, I sort of "conveniently forgot" about the debt. Some would regard that as pretty damn sleazy, but I'd sent most of my army pay to my ever-loving unfaithful wife. Frenchie was a crazy kind of guy, with more guts and meanness inside him than a barrel of rattlesnakes. Even if he did nearly get us killed on a couple of his wild excursions, he was still the king of cribbage.

Oh well, I'd probably never see him again anyhow.

The long awaited announcement finally came loud and clear over the intercom: "All troops prepare to board busses for Bien Hoa Airfield." What a glorious sound, what a great feeling. At last, I was almost out of this hellhole.

On the road to the airfield was a cluster of signs nailed to a large wooden post that I'd driven by many times before. They all pointed in the same direction and indicated homeward bound destinations: California, U.S.A.; Pittsburgh, 10270 miles; New Orleans, 11568 miles; Des Moines, 9555 miles and Mobile, Alabama. All places familiar to American troops, these signs gave us something to look forward to.

At the airfield terminal, the intercom voice announced that our freedom flight was arriving in fifteen minutes. A few of us headed out on the hot tarmac and waited, trying to get an early, distant glimpse of our plane. We'd watched these aircraft come and go so many times before. In Nam there wasn't much else to keep your morale up, so just seeing one of these beautiful American freedom birds gave us a warm feeling inside. And now it was our turn to fly out. The anticipation was so strong, we could practically taste it.

Our flight to the world would be on a F.T.A., Flying Tiger Airlines, or, as we all dubbed it, "the army airlines." Flying Tiger was mainly an airfreight carrier that converted several of their jets to passenger airlines, but what the hell did we care so long as it took us home.

We watched intently as the big, beautiful jet landed and taxied down the long airstrip and eventually stopped just out in front of us on the tarmac. We all watched patiently as new replacement recruits streamed off the plane and down the long flight of stairs. They wore their stateside khaki uniforms, all neat and clean. Many of the seasoned troops, including myself, in our faded green combat jungle fatigues, greeted and shook hands with the new guys and wished them well as they filed past, heading for the terminal.

While waiting our turn to board the big jet, I struck up a conversation with one of the many airfield guards, a talkative fellow. "You guys are sure darn lucky today," he said, "But I'll be out of here in forty-one more days. I'm gettin' real short, short, short, hallelujah!" A typical feeling; we all wanted out of Nam.

As we stood watching the new recruits shuffle by, I noticed a large stack of elongated aluminum boxes stacked up outside the terminal on the hot tarmac. I knew what they were: morgue boxes. And I noticed a smell I had detected before, during the time I drove my bus to Bien Hoa Airfield. A familiar odor that seemed to be emanating from the boxes. I asked the airfield guard about it.

"Embalming fluid," he replied, "Used to preserve the bodies and body parts in all those reusable morgue boxes. What you're looking at is the sad end of the line for the guys that didn't make it." As I stood there staring at the boxes he went on with, "The goddamned sons-a-bitchin' Charlies ruined their trip home to the world. You guys are the lucky ones. And you know, those bastard Viet Cong and NVA are always trying to bust us up or blow our asses off here at the big field, so I hope when my day comes I'll be lucky, just like you guys."

I hoped he would. Sure, the damn Charlies were directly responsible for so many thousands of deaths. But how about those bastards back home who got us into this useless mess in the first place?

The black tarmac had got damn hot that afternoon and we couldn't wait to get seated in the freedom bird. Finally, the announcement we'd all been patiently waiting for came over a bullhorn, and we formed a line and headed out to the plane and up the same long stairs that the new replacement recruits had walked down an hour before.

At the top of the stairway I paused for a moment and looked back one last time. A short glance to say farewell to this hostile, war-ravaged country. Though I didn't physically wave or salute, my mind was doing just that.

Inside, we were greeted by one of several smiling, young and beautiful round-eyed hostesses. What a great feeling to see lovely American women again. Their wonderful smiles and the smell of their perfume brought back sweet memories. Though we'd climbed the stairs to heaven there was still something troubling me: what was I to do about my wife when I got home? Still, I didn't want to spoil this treasured moment; I had to put my problems with Karen on the back burner for the time being, so I could absorb the tremendous joy of getting my ass out of Vietnam.

Shortly after settling into one of the plush seats, I asked one of the sweet smelling hostesses, "How long will it be before we get to the world. . . I'm sorry, I mean, California?"

"Approximately eighteen total hours with all the stops, refueling and such, sir," she smiled.

"Thank you very much," I replied. Then I thought, no one, but no one in this man's army has ever called me 'sir.' For regular grunts like me, receiving any kind of respect was most unusual. Especially from the lifers. But here was this hostess, just acting normal and courteous. What a change; I'd almost forgotten what the real world was like.

The four big engines were now screaming as the jet streaked down the long runway. The 707 lifted off. Out my window I saw an infantryman, an airfield security guard, whip a quick salute to the climbing jet. He was probably thinking it would be his turn before long. For some, today meant home. For others, it was just the beginning. And for too damn many, it was the sad end.

Now, on a flight headed back to the world, I began to feel very secure, a feeling I hadn't had for such a long time. I was finally out of harms way. It was almost the feeling a small child gets when he or she is scratched or banged up after falling off a bicycle, then running to mother's arms for love and security.

We'd been in the air an hour or so and I desperately needed to relieve myself. My bladder was about to runneth over due to all the excitement (and downing a few sodas at the terminal). As I headed down the aisle toward the restroom, a familiar face caught my eye. The soldier was sitting on the inside seat, next to the aisle. I immediately recognized his slime ball face, that of the goddamn lifer First Sergeant Bruno, the son-of-a-bitch who canned me from my bus driver's job. Well if that doesn't beat all, I thought to myself. If this rotten bastard had had his way, I might be inside one of those aluminum morgue boxes right now, on the way back home to push up the daisies.

He actually made brief eye contact, but I don't believe he recognized me. He obviously couldn't. He didn't have enough gray matter to even accomplish that! Or was he perhaps just "faking me out?" Or did he simply not want to convey the impression that he knew me, because of the very real possibility that I might bust his chops? (I sure wanted to, but I doubt that I'd actually have done it.)

I couldn't believe it; what the hell were the odds that this lifer would be on my flight to freedom? I walked right past him and into the restroom, pissed completely off even before I got to the pisser. Then I thought, don't let this dude ruin your trip. Just forget the son-of-a-bitchin' fireplug of a man, he's a lost cause. He was probably born into the army and doesn't know any other way to behave.

I entered the cramped restroom, unbuttoned my jungle fatigues and started to take a relieving piss in this goofy looking toilet. To my horror, there was a sticky, yellowish trace of puss in my white boxer shorts. I looked more closely. Oh, my God, I've got the clap! And I'm only a day or two from seeing my wife! What should I do? I was screwed, was my first thought. Then I started to wonder why, after what I was sure Karen had been up to, I should even give a damn. For my own sake, though, I knew that as soon as I got to the Oakland Army Center I'd have to consult a doctor. But for now, I decided to try to enjoy the rest of the flight and attempt to forget the slimly little first sergeant. And the possible V.D. Easier said then done, but I stuck it out.

Sixteen hours later, after a quick refueling in Anchorage, Alaska, we landed at California's Travis Air Force Base.

We taxied in and the jet stopped at the terminal area. Looking out the window, I noticed a group of hippie-looking young people; long hair, tie-dyed colorful clothes and such. Flower children. I figured they were going to give us some kind of welcoming party. Several hand-lettered signs featured vulgar and despicable words like "Baby Butchers," "Baby Killers," "War Mongers," "Make Love Not War," and "Love and *Piece*." Clearly, the dumbo holding that sign meant "Love and Peace," not, "Love and Piece." Then again, with their free love spirit, maybe that's exactly what he meant. My take was that these were a bunch of crazy-acting degenerates.

Airport security was trying to keep the protesters in some sort of order, but many were unruly and threw eggs, tomatoes and other fruits or vegetables at us. Most of us elected to run for the terminal rather than walk, but we had to go right through the middle of a large group of these bastards, many of them screaming vulgar language as we got closer, and continuing to throw all kinds of stuff. A troop in front of me went after one of the longhairs who had splattered him with a raw egg. Though none of us were injured, we had to dodge their barrage of produce, and it certainly didn't make for a great welcome home.

Many of us were shook up and pissed off, but compared to what we had had to contend with in Vietnam, this was mild. Actually, compared to the fear, danger and bullshit we'd been through, it was a piece of cake. Most of us shook it off like water off a duck's back, got our shit together and waited for our bus to the Oakland Army Center.

While I'd always had serious reservations about America's involvement in Vietnam, and doubted that the tens of thousands of young Americans who came back in those reusable morgue boxes was anything but a tragic waste of life, I certainly didn't believe that those who "greeted" us needed to lay on additional hardships. Protesting the war was one thing, but harassing returning GIs was seriously outrageous and completely uncalled for. I mean, we had enough troubles already.

August 1, 1969. United States Army Personnel Center, Oakland, California. The mess hall.

For most of us, this would be our last army meal. The chow line moved fairly fast, and after so-so food on the long flight home we all craved something special.

Well, it wasn't half bad. In fact, I was somewhat surprised; a T-bone steak dinner with all the fixins, a darn good meal by army standards. For once, it seemed as if we were being treated with a little respect. I guess you had to earn your last meal in this man's army. Thank you, Uncle Sam! Of course, maybe it just tasted so good because I was on American soil.

As I was eating, I happened to look over and notice that cocky, sawed-off bottom feeder, First Sergeant Bruno again. He was the kind of lifer that would piss off the pope. Every time I saw him I thought about his "short man" syndrome, his shitty and arrogant attitude. If I could only meet him in a dark alley. That feeling of wanting to bust him in the chops surfaced again, but I restrained myself. (Over and over again while in Nam, I'd had to restrain myself from cold-cocking some self-centered lifer.) Physical or even verbal abuse at this late date could get me into a peck of trouble, and that was something I didn't need. So I bit my tongue, pushed the anger out of my head, finished the meal and directed my thoughts toward my medical condition. Especially checking out the possible V.D.

And I began to focus on Karen too. I had called her from Anchorage, so she knew I'd be in Oakland. I had made up the excuse that the army doctors were very concerned about my gut, and wanted me to stay over for a thorough physical. In reality, I needed to address my damned dick-drip problem.

After dinner, I went to my assigned barracks, a huge place and mostly empty except for a half-dozen black troops. Having had run-ins with a couple black guys before, I decided to play it safe and selected a bunk at the opposite end of the barracks. These black troops were on their way to Nam, and it seemed like they gave me some respect, since I was just back from my tour. They didn't say much as they walked back and forth to their bunks. Nor did I, and that was just fine, I didn't need any hassles. Though it was against my nature to be unsociable to another human being of any race or religion, the simple fact was that during the 60s and 70s there seemed to be a fair amount of racism, discrimination and animosity between black and white troops.

The next morning, I went to the dispensary and was

thoroughly examined by a couple of army doctors. They looked over my extensive medical history then both doctors and I sat down to discuss my intestinal disorder and skin rashes. And I brought up the urinary discharge that I was terribly worried about. One of the docs ran a scan of the discharge and checked the specimen. The results came back negative for V.D. – which was a *positive* for me!

"Then what the hell's wrong with me?" I asked.

"You have a urinary infection called nonspecific urethritis," said the first doc. "It's not V.D., so don't worry about it."

What a relief! I'd been scared to death.

He gave me some antibiotics to take care of the infection. Then we talked about the gut stuff. "Quite a few of your physical and mental problems are probably caused from severe stress," said the other doc. "It's called Transient Situation Disturbance. It's a war-related health problem." (Years later, they'd rename it PTSD, Post Traumatic Stress Disorder.)

Then I told the doctors about my unfaithful wife.

"One way or the other," the second doc said, "You need to minimize your hard feelings and the mental stress associated with her. That will be the first step toward healing your body and nervous system."

After the visit I called Karen. Miraculously, she wasn't busy. Gee whiz! (I guess it was my lucky day. And yes, I'm being sarcastic.) Within four hours she arrived at the Oakland Army Center. She was still as beautiful as I'd remembered her. We greeted one another cheerily, but there were obviously many reservations on both our parts. Much unsaid.

In the car on the way home, I found myself wondering what the hell our future would bring.

IT'S HOW WE SAY IT

"WE SET UP OUR NDP NEAR WHERE THE LRP'S HAD SPOTTED VC THE DAY BEFORE. THE FAC HAD THE AREA POUNDED PRETTY HARD, BUT ON A MORNING SRP WE FOUND SO MANY CHARLIES WE NEARLY RAN OUT OF AMMO. BUT THANKS TO A LOG BIRD WE WERE REALLY ABLE TO ZAP THEM. THE RTO CALLED FOR ARTY AND GUNSHIPS, AND GHOST RIDER DIRECTED REINFORCEMENTS FROM HIS C&C SLICK. WE DIDN'T NEED A SINGLE DUSTOFF."

To help your family and friends understand you when you return home, we offer this list of terms and their definitions, most of which belong exclusively to the U.S. soldier in Vietnam.

AMMO—Ammunition.

ARTY—Artillery.

ARVN—Army of the Republic of Vietnam.

BABY-SAN—Vietnamese infant, girl or young lady.

BOONIES—Areas uninhabited by man.

BRING SMOKE—To destroy the enemy.

C & C—Command and control.

CAYUSE—Type of small reconnaissance helicopter (OH-6A).

CHARLIE—The enemy.

CHINOOK—Type of large transport helicopter (CH-47A & B).

CHOPPER—Helicopter.

COBRA—Type of gunship (AH-1G)

COMMO—Communications.

DUSTOFF—Medical evacuation by helicopter.

FDC—Fire direction center (for mortars and artillery).

FO—Forward observer (calls in artillery strikes).

GHOST RIDER, RED INDIAN, ETC.—In casual conversation, usually the code name for an officer above the rank of major.

GRUNT—Infantryman.

GUNSHIP—Armed helicopter (AH-1G or UH-1A).

HARD HAT—Main Force Viet Cong soldier.

HOOK—See Chinook.

HOOCH—Sleeping quarters.

HUEY—Helicopter (UH-1).

HUMP—To indulge in strenuous activity—e.g., hump ammo, hump the boonies.

LAW—Light anti-tank weapon.

LOG BIRD—Resupply helicopter.

LP—Listening post.

LRP—Long range patrol.

LZ—Landing zone.

MAMA-SAN—Elderly Vietnamese woman.

MEDEVAC—Medical evacuation helicopter.

NDP—Night defensive position.

NVA—North Vietnamese Army.

PAPA-SAN—Elderly Vietnamese man.

PSYOPS—Psychological operations.

ROUGH-PUFF (RF/PF)—South Vietnamese Regional or Popular forces soldier.

SLICK—Unarmed or lightly armed helicopter (UH-1D).

SPOOKY—Night reconnaissance aircraft (USAF C-47 or DC-3).

SRP—Short range patrol.

VC—Viet Cong.

ZAP—To hit with a bullet.

SUMMER, 1969

27

I'D LEARNED THE LANGUAGE OF THE ARMY,
NOW I'D HAVE TO LEARN THE LAY OF THE LAND AT HOME

YEAR 1980. ME AND MARCY (MY THIRD WIFE) TOP RIGHT
THE TROUT HATCHERY.

DECADES

Time is a companion that goes with us on a journey. It reminds us

to cherish each moment, because it will never come again. What we

leave behind is not as important as how we have lived.

Captain Jean-Luc Picard (Patrick Stewart), in Star Trek, Generations

I LOOK BACK on the twenty-seven years between August of 1969 when Karen picked me up at the Oakland Army Center, and the chilly afternoon in January of 1996 when I found myself in almost total collapse in front of the Vietnam Veterans Memorial in DC, as something of a whirlwind. To this day, I'm not sure how much of what I went through was directly related to Vietnam, and how much was just some kind of inborn combination of crazy, mixed up chemistry.

The emotional hurt I'd endured over Karen never went away. As I discovered not too long after coming home, sometime after I'd left for Nam she'd taken up with the twenty-year-old brother of an Air Force troop I'd met over there. This brother showing up at our place – which Karen told me were "visits" to our young daughter – seemed way out of place and totally weird. A twenty-year-old getting off on visiting a baby? Come on! With me working four consecutive twenty-four hour shifts at the California Division of Forestry's fire station in Sutter Hill again, and often unable to reach Karen by phone (because she either wasn't home or didn't answer) and with her treating me like dirt under her feet when I was around the house, I became more and more whacked out and very suspicious. After weeks of nervous exhaustion over her evasions, excuses and another outright lie after arriving home from my shift one day about her young friend "visiting the baby," I finally told her, "That's it. I'm out of here!"

Two weeks later, after I'd moved out and filed for divorce, some friends, Fred and Rita, tried to get us together again.[1] They showed up with wine, cheese, and friendly faces – and with Karen, in the back seat of Fred's car. Karen leaned out the back window, apologized for not sending me many letters in Nam, and said, "but I want you to know I really haven't been messin' around on you at all."

I looked at her in a fairly disgusted way and said nothing. Maybe, if either of us had known how to sit quietly, just talk things out in a straightforward way and put the past behind us, we could have learned how to live together. Maybe; I'm not sure. But that never happened. My own hurt was too great, and Karen was clearly headed in her own direction.

"Haven't been messin' around," she'd said. I sure as hell wanted to fall for her sweet sales pitch, because my love for her had been something powerful. But my better judgment told me not to tumble, so I took a rain check on the day out. Then, as Fred and Rita drove off, Karen looked at me through the back window of the car. Watching her disappear from my life left me with a dreadfully dreary and terribly empty feeling. She was

---

[1] Fred was the good soldier buddy at Fort Hood, Texas who procrastinated with the orders about my being shipped to Vietnam (Chapter 5).

such a beautiful woman, I thought. A real beauty queen. But her lying eyes sang a very different song. As the three of them drove around the turn and down Ridge Road and out of sight, my heart sank to the tips of my toes, and tears began streaming down my face.[2]

In terms of work, it didn't take me long to remind myself of the blatant arrogance, ignorance, and disrespectful ordering around that had been dished out by many of my superiors at my CDF fire truck driving job when I'd worked there before Vietnam. I came back to the same set of circumstances. The mindset was totally military, an outrageous and completely uncalled for ranking system. I'd be, for example, ordered by an overzealous, power hungry egomaniacal assistant forest ranger, to put out some tiny distant ember, flame, or wisp of smoke, smack dab in the middle of a 500-acre burn that had already been extinguished. Or, when the brass showed up when we weren't particularly busy, I'd be told to grab a screwdriver or some other damn close by device, and make like I was doing something. Surprisingly, some wimpy employees terrified of losing their jobs went along with this childish phony baloney work habits and ordering about. But not me. It felt exactly like I was back in the Army, with pompous bosses getting their jollies off by picking on or belittling lower ranking firemen. And I was often the one on the receiving end. Enough bullshit, I finally decided. I quit and never looked back, and have been self-employed ever since.

For more years after the divorce than I like to recall, I was on a rampage. Boozy binges and getting gals into bed. Plenty of them. It became an obsession, chasing and using women for phony love affairs or selfish sexual

---

[2] This encounter took place at the junction of Bowman Road and Ridge Road, two miles west of Pine Grove, California. (Bowman Road is named after Ivan and Georgia Bowman, my mom and dad, the original owners and developers of Sunset Heights. And all three sons have roads within the tract named after them - Marc Drive, Steven Lane and Lynn Way.)

desire. Fat women, skinny women, tall or short, married or not, redheads, blondes and brunets, it didn't matter. Though I had my druthers on who was attractive, most of the time I didn't care. All I was after was a good lay. I was (I thought) just having fun, going along for the ride, with my dick doing the driving.

In Vietnam, though I'd caught the clap a couple times, I had also decided that once out of that hellhole I was going to get my fair share of the good stuff. And Karen, I assumed, would be the sole object of my affection. Wrong. Damn wishful thinking. So every time I'd come across some stuck-up, prick-teasing hard-bodied beauty playing the hard-to-get program, I'd think about Karen and go after her hot and heavy, like I was getting a kind of perverted revenge on my former wife. Tell 'em lies, use 'em up, spit 'em out and move on, that seemed to be my MO. Not something I look back on with the slightest pride, but it was what it was.

All this time I was being a son-of-a-bitch toward women, the grief and anger over my unfaithful ex-wife continued tormenting me. (Though I was never violent, I probably did push the envelope a bit and was verbally abusive on a couple occasions.) I'd constantly flash back to those long nights lying in my bunk at Bien Hoa, the mental anguish over not hearing from her. It seemed like it would never go away. The more I thought about it, the more women I'd go after, and the more I'd wake up depressed after some all night binge. Even got into LSD once. And with the gal who turned me on to it, spent the night and most of the next day screwing like there *was* no next day. Another time, I set up a trusting gal who was sweet on me with a "spin the bottle" game at our local Bowman Realty office near where I lived in the Sierra foothills. (I'd become a licensed realtor by now, and was making a half-ass living selling land and houses.) My clever plan – a demented plan, as I look back on it – was to get her drunk, talk her into getting naked with a tricky spin of the bottle, then have her pleasure a good friend of mine, Gary, who I figured needed a great lay. Didn't quite work out that way. Drunk as she got, and naked as she did get, peeling off one garment after another, she adamantly refused to take on my buddy, and insisted on paying her sexual debt only with me. Finally, around midnight, and while she was in the bathroom, my pal grabbed her clothes and dumped them smack dab in the middle of State Highway 88 running through Pine Grove (a main route to South Lake Tahoe) outside the office. After she pleaded for us to get her clothes back, and after again refusing to service my friend, the two of us staggered out of the office, leaving her there. "Generously," we pointed to the highway and said, "You'll find your clothes out on the road."

Later, when we returned to lock the office, we found that she'd slipped away into the night buck naked, retrieved her clothes some damn way, and skedaddled home.

One fine summer evening, I took a favorite girlfriend, Marcy Doran (later to be my third wife), out for drinks at a local foothills tavern, Big Art's, in the town of Pine Grove. Low and behold, in came my ex, Karen, with her new boyfriend, Dave, another Vietnam vet, big and brassy, a smart-ass with a big mouth and a violent reputation. He'd usually pick on some poor drunk slob half his size and smash the guy's face in when he least expected it.

Well, after crazy Dave and Karen invited themselves to the table where Marcy and I were sitting, and after he'd rubbed it in my face several times that he was with my ex (still one of the best looking women I knew), and after both of us had become pretty well juiced – and after Dave had started dancing with Marcy and pawing her everywhere he could, I had had enough. In minutes, we were into it, and seconds later I had him bleeding, dizzy and delirious. Finally, after being pulled off the bastard by friends, then having cleaned myself up in the nearby real estate office, I decided to go after him again. I wanted to finish this business, rearrange his face in such a manner that he'd never pull anything like this again. But big Dave, holed up in the bar, had had enough and wouldn't come out.

Even after all that I couldn't get Karen's treatment of me while I was in Nam out of my head. There I'd been, locked down in a goofed up war, but still "defending my country," while she'd been living it up at home, getting it on with some twenty-year-old (and others, for all I knew). The images in my brain never let up, and it drove me nuts. On the other hand, I'd never had anything specific on her, just rumor, speculation, and her rotten behavior toward me. But then one day the whole thing came to a head and a hot boil. One of my good buddies told me that while I was in Nam he'd once spotted Karen banging away in my green 1967 Buick Special with this punk brother of the Air Force dude I had had a few beers with in Nam. That did it. That was the crusher. And even though I had no thought of getting Karen back, and didn't even care that much anymore, I let myself be talked into going after this dude. Being young bucks, I guess we all needed some excitement.

The next afternoon, me and three other buddies cornered him on a Sierra foothills side road and forced his pickup to pull over. His sister was with him, and when it became clear what we were up to, he climbed out, and with his smart mouth threatened to call the cops. Well, his sister started yelling and screaming and waving her arms around. And after the punk basically lied about not balling my wife – which we all knew was a barefaced lie – one of my buddies, Larry, pushed a half full Oly beer can straight into his face. Then, with a set of brass knuckles on his right hand, he hauled off and busted the poor bastard in the chops. With him laying on the ground, bleeding, whimpering and pleading for mercy, and his sister continuing to holler bloody murder, I told Larry, "That's enough, he's had it." So we split. The dude was shaken, and pretty roughed up, but nothing too serious.

Two months later, I was summoned to appear in the Amador County Superior Court in the city of Jackson. The charge: assault and battery. I was fined $1000 and got two years probation. My coconspirators, Larry, Gary and Doug, simply got probation. Got to admit, it was a costly, harebrained idea. Still, at the time it made me feel a little better. I figured that jerk got what he deserved.

Between numerous one-night stands, barfly binges and escapades, short and long-term live-ins and shackup jobs, I even tried marriage again. Caught up in a mixture of imaginary love affairs, depression, booze binges galore, and with no salvation in sight but with a cockeyed attempt to return to some kind of normalcy, I plunged into wedded bliss with Marcy (the cute gal I was with when I tore into big Dave at Big Art's Tavern). Caring and companionship, plus three square meals a day, I thought, would help mend my physical and emotional wounds. Never happened. Though Marcy was a lovable and caring person, and though I probably tried the best I knew how (which didn't amount to much) to be a decent husband, I couldn't pull it off. Before long, I resumed my previous behavior: adulterous affairs, prowling bars and nightclubs for available women, and more binge drinking.

Even without a knock down, drag out affair, we were soon divorced. Amicably, this time, with Marcy and me somehow remaining good friends to this day. I'm sure she didn't enjoy my crazy antics, but she never held a grudge, and seemed to understand why I had so many demons tormenting me.

And wouldn't you know, before long I was married

yet again! With the same scenario, an attempt to pull myself out of the deep hole of despondency and despair I'd fallen into. But this time, there was a difference. The tables were turned. I was the victim.

Sally was her name. Younger than me by several years. Though my love for her was at best marginal, this fourth marriage, rocky from the start, produced two wonderful children who I dearly loved.[3] And, mainly because of the children, I genuinely tried to make the marriage work.

By now, in spite of the emotional edge I was coasting along on, I was also putting most of my time and energy into starting businesses, buying and developing property, and stuffing money into the bank. After several years of tossing around cash like it was going out of style and living on a financial precipice, by now I was actually doing quite well.

But it didn't matter. Nothing seemed to pan out right. The more money I brought in, the more Sally squandered. And over time I discovered that, just like me, Sally had been having adulterous affairs. To top it off, one evening, while she and I and a longtime buddy since high school – he was also a partner with me in a logging business – were enjoying cocktails in our hot tub, she started to engage in an outrageous sex act with him. I got out of the tub and retreated to the house, steaming. And almost did the unthinkable, because thoughts of blowing them both away with one of my guns – or maybe crushing their skulls with a Louisville Slugger – ran through my head. Though gradually (and grudgingly) I let the incident go and forgave her – she was, after all, fairly plastered – the partnership with my buddy was immediately dissolved.

Also gradually, it became crystal clear that Sally had

[3]Their names are Amanda and Blake; named after the talented actress Amanda Blake (Miss Kitty) on the old Gunsmoke television series.

from day one been on a mission: to stack our financial deck completely in her own favor. Naively, and too busy working at my logging business to notice what was going on, I had placed all my trust in my new wife and let her manage our assets. Completely unbeknown to me, Sally had drained our joint bank accounts of over $20,000 and stashed all of that, my hard-earned cash, in her own hidden accounts scattered here and there over three western states! She even forged my name on an additional $18,000 worth of checks that had been sent to me for the sale of a small California property I owned, and spent every nickel. As soon as her John Hancock was on the title to a big ranch I'd acquired in Montana, as well as on titles to the rest of my properties – totaling over a million dollars in value – she filed for divorce.

After the smoke had cleared from this fourth divorce, I had been picked clean. I found out that she'd even had the gall to put her mother's two vehicles on our Montana ranch insurance (the cars had never left California). And while preparing to burn debris one day, I discovered many canceled checks made out to several of Sally's friends and relatives. With the connivance of a Montana lawyer and judge I was sure were in cahoots, most of the property I'd acquired, most of my liquid assets, and most precious to me of all, my two dear children, were taken away. To this day I'm still digging out of that financial hole. And the emotional toll took years to get over.

A damn hard lesson learned. But thank God she was gone!

The other side of this almost three decades-long, crazy, sordid and peculiar coin that was my life after Vietnam, had to do with the many business ventures I got into. And more specifically how, in one way or another, they all kind of tied in to the bureaucracy, regulation and giant egos I got to know so well during the war. It was sort of like the military mindset had simply been transferred to civilian life. These examples will give you an idea:

Even before Nam, I'd had a distinct fascination with the outdoors. My father and brothers and I had always loved hunting, fishing, and nature in general. As early as 1966 I'd become interested in rearing trout and salmon as a business. Then, after my army discharge, when my mother purchased two hundred acres in California's Calaveras County, on a lovely tributary of the nearby Mokelumne River (called the Licking Fork) running through the middle, I immediately envisioned a trout hatchery on the property. With mom's approval, by the spring of 1973 I began construction, and within two years we had an impressive operation going: the Blue Mountain Trout Hatchery. We had ponds brimming with trout, markets to sell the fish too, certified, disease-free trout eggs being shipped all over the United States, and fishermen streaming in from nearby counties to catch trophy-sized rainbows and golden-bow trout in special ponds and the beautiful stream.[4]

Business was swimming along nicely.

But then the trouble started. Contrary to the law, a neighboring rancher refused to do anything about his cattle trampling across our land, eating and scattering trout feed everywhere and spewing slimy manure all over the place. And the local animal control and sheriff's department (after promising to rectify the situation) ultimately did nothing. By now, I'd become irate over the rude intrusion of these munching moochers. The hatchery had been pristine and park-like, but who in their right mind would want to fish or enjoy a peaceful picnic accompanied by the constant lowing of cattle and a meadow literally doused with varying degrees of wet and dry cow dung? Very appealing, right? Wrong!

---

[4] Golden-bow were a new strain, which, through breeding experiments, I'd developed by crossing rainbows with golden trout.

So I had to take matters into my own hands. One day, absolutely furious when a pair of marauding cows got into one of the raceway ponds, totally freaking the fish and breaking dam boards and screens and spilling and splashing trout everywhere, I shot and then butchered both of them. Well that brought in the law. Local cops and sheriff's deputies swarmed all over, searching, threatening and grilling me, but they never found a shred of evidence. (We'd stowed the meat in a friend's cooler in his barn.)

That was the beginning. Then, after a severe drought in 1976 and 1977, I lost all my trophy trout. In the fall of 1977 the entire stream dwindled to a trickle of fifty gallons per minute. It took three years to recover. And in 1980, during weeks when it rained buckets, I lost most of my trout eggs and fingerlings. Silt-filled water caused by an upstream lumber company that had – completely contrary to California forest practice rules – previously terraced their hillsides with bulldozers for new tree plantings, flooded our property. Though the company paid off, the years of hassles with the neighbor's cows, plus the womanizing and boozing I still hadn't escaped from, sent me into another emotional tailspin.

Then, one morning after I'd brought the hatchery back up to par, as I was making my normal feeding rounds and cleaning fish screens, I noticed that some of the trout were acting very peculiar. Within a few days after my concerned phone call, a local biologist, John Modin, came out, netted several specimens and examined them at his lab. Turned out that the fish had come down with a debilitating illness called "whirling" disease. After a long battle with the California Department of Fish and Game, and even though not all the fish were affected, the Department came in with bulldozing equipment, loaders and dump trucks, and over a period of two weeks filled in every damn pond. After the government boys got through screwing with the place, it looked like a moonscape. My mother, disbelieving, stood there one day in shock and dismay, the tears streaming down her face. And I wasn't happy over the entire ordeal myself.

They did say I could keep what trout eggs I had in my incubators, and that after the hatchlings were proven disease free I could start again. How generous! But that was it; every live fish had to go. (Though I was allowed to give away or sell some, since the disease couldn't be spread to humans.) And I was told not to sell or plant any fish for "live stocking purposes."

What really tore me apart was the discovery that someone had been spreading an ugly, unfounded rumor that I had picked up diseased trout somewhere, and that's how my stock had become infected. The rumor, started I believe by some dimwit at the California Department of Fish and Game, sounded credible to some. But it was garbage. I had raised every fish myself and had no need to acquire outside trout. In fact, a few state-owned *California* fisheries later came down with the same disease. (Whirling disease.) But when that happened, the Fish and Game officials hushed it up, maintaining the fiction that the state owned hatcheries were "pure," while mine was "diseased." Of course, not a single state hatchery was ever shut down, and they swept their dirty little secret under the carpet.

By now, with the losses I'd suffered, my cash flow was zilch. Finally, after a gazillion letters and phone calls, the state was forced to partially compensate me for my losses. Then, after they'd "promised" I could keep and hatch the million plus trout eggs, and after several tests over several months, with not a single "whirling" disease spore found in any of my fingerlings, Fish and Game decided "not to take any chances," and forced me to euthanize every last one of the poor creatures. Everyone covers his ass. Just like in Nam.

I had to destroy a million fingerlings! Which happened to be completely healthy. And the only way to do this quickly was to cut off the flow and let the remaining water drain from the troughs that held them. Asphyxiation. Doing this simply added another spoke to the wheel of everlasting bitterness I felt toward out of control, insidious and overflowing government. It was such a sad, disgusting and heart-wrenching experience. Cruel, inhumane and as barbaric as it gets. And you can imagine the psychic devastation. This nearly destroyed me, and the anger and pain and emotional scars continue to this day.

Overlapping the decline and eventual death of my trout hatchery, I opened a seafood market and deli, Sierra Seafood. With the thousand pounds of trout that Fish and Game "generously" allowed me to keep, I had a great start. Actually, I decided to give them away at my grand opening. I also created a "secret recipe" for clam chowder that locals couldn't get enough of. With fresh crab salads, crab and shrimp cocktails, and a variety of other delicacies, Sierra Seafood was an instant success; even with some of the cheapskate mountain folk expecting quality saltwater dishes and seafood purchases at hot dog prices. And even in spite of the crazy Italian owner of an adjoining feed store (another Vietnam vet, he said) constantly gagging us with the big diesel rig he kept running for hours on end right next door.

But then, the good old boy network reared its ugly head again. This time, in the form of a group of Northern California fisherman who wanted to monopolize the wholesale fish supply operation in their neck of the woods. My brother Steve, trying to recover from his own emotional scars after Vietnam, plus a business partnership gone sour – and partially to supply Sierra Seafood – had started a new venture in Crescent City, buying fish from local Vietnam vets who were also commercial fisherman. But after he and a bunch of the vets put up a good fight, city fathers and a local warehouse owner forced him to knuckle under to their thinly disguised hints that unless he folded his tent, dire consequences would result. I mean, there was a strong probability of mafia-like connections among that fishing community. With Steve no longer able to supply me, and with another wholesaler soon raising his prices, the black clouds of failure were looming on the horizon again.

And then, Sierra Seafood burned to the ground! (And the Italian's feed store too.)

Arson! screamed my old bosses and coworkers at the California Department of Forestry. Arson! screamed headlines in the local press. Arson! screamed the local police and fire officials. I was called in for questioning, and pressured to submit to a lie detector. (On an attorney's advice, who said I had no legal obligation to take it, I never even showed up for the test.) Of course, since I'd done nothing, they had nothing on me. How the fire started remained a mystery. And eventually, I accepted an apparently generous but wholly inadequate insurance settlement.

By now, the whole experience had me worn out and burned to a cinder. Also by now, I'd lost interest in the fish market, and the easiest course was to return to my old routine of womanizing and booze. Same old story.

With the insurance money, I bought a Caterpillar logging bulldozer and log loader. For several years, I made a decent success of this, logging small and large properties, as well as land I'd buy that had marketable timber. And then (what else is new) I got into trouble again. This time with a local lumber mill that agreed to put up $50,000 in front money toward the purchase of twenty acres of land I figured I could log $200,000 worth of timber from. Not too damn bad, I thought, for just a couple months work. After all was said and done, and with the loan paid off, I figured I'd wind up with at least $125,000 in my pocket. Before signing the contract I checked it out with a logger friend, Tom Ide,who warned me that though the contract looked OK, the mill had a sleazy reputation, often cheating timber operators like me.

So, on Tom's say so, I backed out of the deal. He said that he'd simply pay off the loan to the lumber mill as well as pay the remaining purchase price on the land, and we'd be in business together. Partners. With him now owning all the timber rights and also one half of the land, he'd be doing the logging and getting all the proceeds from the timber sale. To tell the truth, the whole deal did sound a bit crazy. I should have known better, but at the time my head was so far up my ass from an absence of careful thinking that I couldn't see the woods for the trees. I gave up all that fine, valuable timber and ended up just owning half interest in the land! I should have had my head examined.

Well, when my partner's $50,000 check got to the lumber mill, the shit hit the fan. The mill called and told me I should forget my deal with him or there'd be legal trouble. They said they'd just chalk it up to a big brain fade on my part.

"Screw the crooked bastards," said my partner, "They're just licking their chops to make a bundle off those twenty acres of beautiful ponderosa pine and sugar pine!"

That had me in a nervous sweat. My deal had been with the mill, not with Tom. And sure enough, as soon as he'd filed a harvest plan and logged the property and pocketed most of the proceeds, along came legal documents aimed at both of us. We were to appear in Amador County Superior Court to answer a suit by the lumber mill about me reneging on the contract.

Do I have to tell you that my partner was found not guilty on all counts? Do I need to mention that the judge threw the book at me? A $20,000 fine! I walked out of the courtroom shaking my head and talking to myself. My "friend" walked off with at least $200,000, plus a half-ownership in the land. To rub salt in my emotional wounds, the California Department of Forestry filed liens against the property for defaulted and delinquent timber taxes that my partner owed on the harvest.

Having (I hoped) learned something about what it meant to be in business with a "good friend," I went back to logging small properties on my own, employing a four-man crew. I wasn't about to give the lumber mill one damn red cent. Then, one day, driving up to my work site (the log landing), I found my Caterpillar dozer gone! Vanished. I went completely bughouse. Turned out that the sheriff's office had seized my equipment as part payment for the lien the court had imposed on me for the lumber mill judgment. The dozer was going up for sale in the county sheriff's auction. This, I knew, would result in another good old boy fix, because it was common knowledge that favorite buddies got dibs on those sales.

After some high class and rather funny shenanigans, in which I snatched the county-seized dozer back, then to my sad disappointment had it confiscated again, it finally landed on the auction block. But do you think I was notified? Do you think I had a chance to buy it back? In your dreams. That ego-driving, backstabbing, back room, conniving, "one hand washes the other" mindset was alive and well and working.

Then, after one of my crew let the top of a ponderosa pine fall into a local river and simply left it there, I was fined. And then an addle-brained Fish and Game warden had me pull out a culvert on my mother's ranch because I'd neglected to file a "stream conversion permit" (there *was* no stream!) And then I got a thirty-day jail sentence for environmental degradation because of the tree-felling incident (which was lowered to twenty days, which I worked off by washing California Highway Patrol cars).[5] To add to the heartbreak, I received an additional thirty-day jail sentence for snatching the dozer and embarrassing a bunch of Calaveras County thugs. But all they could charge me with was breaking a court order, and the sentence was reduced to twenty days, which I happily worked off by brush clearing and policing county road rights of way. (We called our road crew the Chain Gang.)

And of course I'd predicted it: the county auctioned off my fine dozer, a $25,000 piece of equipment, for a pitiful $6000.

Too often, my decades after Vietnam felt like I was living the whole damn war over again. But this time with my fellow citizens, or in confrontation with some occasional demented fellow vet, or with local or state government I thought was supposed to help and protect, and that I'd consistently supported with my taxes. (Most of the time.) The good old boy government network was alive and well. Doing secret favors, I suspect, for their favorite buddies. How different was this than dealing with some hard-ass lifer sergeant or second lieutenant? Sometimes it seemed like the war was still going on. I mean, who *was* my enemy? Was some of it my own doing? I'm still trying to puzzle that out. What do you think?

JANUARY 1996. I'm still at the Wall, waiting for Janet. Scanning the names, remembering fallen comrades, and thinking back on all those years of both great and not so good and some downright half-baked business decisions, confused thinking about women and relationships, and massive hassles with military and a slew of petty bureaucrats. Did I learn anything from it all? I hope so. For sure, I never really learned to make the sys-

---

[5] This was a minor violation; only about ten feet of the top of the pine had fallen into the south fork of the Mokelumne River.

tem work for me. Too often, I went off half-cocked, flew by the seat of my pants and just jumped into bed or into business deals on the basis of some momentary impulse. Not exactly a great way to live a life, is it?

And yet, I thought, as Janet, flashing her generous smile suddenly appeared and waved to me as she returned to the Wall, there had been much to appreciate and a lot to celebrate.

I was finally able to maintain a solid friendship with my kids.

Brother Steve is now living a fairly normal life with his wife near Sacramento. Every now and then he's had to deal with a bout of nervous stress, but exercise and an occasional antidepressant mostly controls it. He's convinced that Vietnam definitely effected his life in many ways, but he's not bitter.

After the seemingly constant bouts with intestinal discomfort, severe cramps, rashes, and getting to the point where I almost didn't care if I lived or died, and after three major nervous breakdowns along the way, I slowly began to come out of it all. Some of that had to do with just getting back to the woods, hunting and fishing with my good old yellow Labrador, Whitey. Much had to do with my mother, Georgia, who helped see me through the worst bouts of depression. A lot had to do with learning to focus on the immediate and the here and now, forgetting the self pity and dwelling just on my nervous system. Getting out into nature helped, taking the time to visually inspect little things; rocks, pebbles, leaves, flowers, ants, birds, bugs, and butterflies. Even clouds in the big blue sky of Montana, and the big stands of Doug fir and ponderosa pine I've long enjoyed living among, have brought a new sense of peace and order to my life.

Over time, this visual concentration on detail on anything to do with nature and the out of doors, plus physical exercise and the deleting of all junk food and caffeine, has taken on a life of its own, and become, I suppose, a sort of subtle therapy. Or maybe it was just that I began to occupy my mind with things outside myself, instead of with the pervasive sense of hopelessness that for far too many years shadowed my existence.

And of course hooking up with Janet again has been a Godsend. A caring and thoughtful and positive person, she's helped to make moving on more than worthwhile. I'm sure that nobody should have to get married five times to discover the right person. But what the hell, it happens. And the idea that you *can* discover the right person and a better way to live is, after all, what's really important.

When Janet returned to the Wall, I felt reluctant to tell her about the near panic I'd been through, about my frantic ordeal and the massive bout with nerves. But that evening, over dinner and a couple glasses of tasty wine at a fine restaurant, I finally let it all come out, telling her how I'd almost lost consciousness, about feeling completely alone, and about how I felt that everything I'd gone through in Vietnam and since, had somehow overwhelmed me, how it had all come home.

"It was such a soul-warming feeling to be close to all those etched names on the Wall," I said, "A sort of feeling that's hard to put into words. I guess you'd call it a sense of brotherhood, a tremendous spiritual connection. A reconciliation, I suppose."

I told her that in spite of the terrible waste I felt the war had been, and in spite of the crazy military mindset over there, I nevertheless felt very honored and enormously proud to be a Vietnam veteran. And it had been a tremendous privilege to rub elbows with such a revered band of heroic warriors. For myself, I hoped that as life continued I could do better in everything I set my mind to.

A cold "Wall" had warmed my heart.

WHO'S MY ENEMY?

When I went back to Vietnam a few years ago I met Gen. Vo Nguyen Giap, the man who engineered the defeat of the French at Dien Bien Phu and then commanded North Vietnamese forces in the war with South Vietnam — and us. He conceded that because of the Ia Drang his plan to cut Vietnam in half and take the capital had been delayed ten years. But then, he chuckled, it didn't make a difference, did it?[1]

JACK SMITH, ABC NEWS CORRESPON-
DENT AND DECORATED VIETNAM COMBAT
VETERAN

---

[1] The battle of Ia Drang Valley, between an estimated 500 Americans and 3500 Vietnamese, between November 13 and 19, 1965, caused 93% American casualties. Specialist 4/C Jack P. Smith caught up in the death trap captured a vivid and shockingly detailed account. Many of Smith's fellow soldiers could not endure the anguish, and several took their own lives because of the horror they witnessed. It was actually less a battle and more of a massacre that wiped out his company. Even Smith admits that there seemed to be no way out of the predicament these soldiers found themselves in.

THE VIETNAM WAR; THIS GI'S VIEW

I am not going to be the first American president to lose a war.

RICHARD NIXON, 1969

All the wrong people remember Vietnam. I think all the people who remember it should forget it, and all the people who forgot it should remember it.

MICHAEL HERR, SCREENWRITER; *FULL METAL JACKET, APOCALYPSE NOW* (NARRATION)

IT'S IMPORTANT TO NOTE that most of my travels in Nam were restricted to a fairly limited area; in and around Corps III, incorporating the Bien Hoa Army Base, Bien Hoa Air Base, Long Binh Army Base, and the cities of Saigon and Bien Hoa. My duties related to "support and logistics." Support: assisting, helping, defending and maintaining military operations. Logistics: procuring, maintaining and transporting military material and personnel.

It's also important to remember that the views I offer come out of my own experience, and may differ from those of fellow veterans. Opinions vary widely on what any one vet thinks about Vietnamese culture or the people themselves. Anyone talking to more than just a few veterans will obviously discover, depending on the vet's particular experience, a lot of mixed feelings in relation to everything related to the war, and whether they felt the war itself was worth fighting. My opinions are my own, and they're fairly strong ones. Much has been written about Vietnam, and much more will certainly be written. But this is my book, my story, and I figure I've used up enough paper to tell it as briefly but as thoroughly as I need to.

More stories, I leave to the next long-winded Vietnam veteran.

Our foot soldiers, both Army and Marines who stalked the villages, jungles and mountains of Vietnam, we called "grunts" or "ground pounders."

Both men and women fighting with the Viet Cong or North Vietnamese Army we called "Charlies," or "gooks," or sometimes "dinks" or "slopes." All were derogatory names, but that's the way it was back then. They were thought of as clearly inferior, not a force to be taken too seriously. One of the absurd myths floating around during the war was that these pint-sized "little people" really had nothing going for them when compared to the might and power of the United States military. After all, we had mortars, howitzers, M48 tanks, Bell UH-1 "Huey" choppers to rake their jungle hideouts with merciless fire, F-4 Phantom fighters with 20 mm cannons and air-to-air missiles, and the B-52 Stratofortress to bomb and napalm them to hell and gone in both North and South Vietnam.

Oh, sure, they had the Soviet MiG-21, and plenty of Chinese and Soviet firepower, but just as often they relied on old, captured Japanese or French or (recently captured) American arms. Or they improvised, and fashioned weapons out of whatever was at hand. Or they'd dig up the nasty Clamore mines we'd planted and turn right around and use them against us.

Besides, weren't we the finest army the world had ever known? Weren't we fighting for freedom? Didn't we have God on our side? It was only a matter of time. No way were they ever going to win.

Just shows what arrogance and dumb-ass thinking will do.

Most of us didn't particularly hate the enemy. In fact, we didn't really know that much about them. And Vietnam didn't seem like a conventional war. We didn't even understand the enemy or his tactics. Because most of us were draftees and not professional soldiers, all we really knew was that we were there to do a job. But we did have an image of the VC and NVA as that of a band of ruthless fanatics. Kind of like the image reported in the news fifteen or so years earlier, when "hordes of screaming Chinese" stormed into Korea in 1951 and 1952 and pushed the U.S. and U.N. forces most of the way back down the peninsula.

But what was it that made the VC and NVA such ferocious and determined fighters? How come they were so much cleverer and successful in winning the support of the Vietnamese than were those in the government of South Vietnam? I've thought about that a lot since the war. At heart, I've come to believe it was because the communists, both north and south were well trained, dedicated proponents of Vietnamese nationalism. They were able to convince hundreds of thousands of Vietnamese that they were fighting for their own country against the American invaders. And I'm sure that that idea won a lot of converts among the villagers and peasants.

I don't believe that powerless and downtrodden people in a third-world country like Vietnam even thought much about what communism was. Just the idea of being able to work their own land; to have foreign oppressors like the Japanese, then the French and their corrupt South Vietnam puppets off their backs, must have seemed tremendously appealing. And then in came another apparent oppressor, the Americans; also supporting the same puppet government. No wonder such vast numbers of Vietnamese were willing to join with the communists in opposing us.

The American military very much underestimated the resilience of the North Vietnamese. As far as the communists were concerned, the battle with the U.S. was simply a continuation of their struggle against French imperialism. Both, they felt, were wars of liberation, wars of attrition that the outsiders could not win. As Ho Chi Minh – who also led the meticulously prepared and rigorous crusade against the French – pointed out, "You can kill ten of my men for every one I kill of yours, but even at those odds, I will win and you will lose."[2]

Before American troops arrived in Vietnam, the Vietnamese had been in some kind of war against feudal lords or foreign invaders for more than two thousand years. This seems to have created a kind of weird but also very stable nervous system among their people. They never really panic. They've had nothing in their history but struggle and war. I came across this time and time again during my service in country. (As for example in my encounter with the knife-toting "rebel" mamasan on the bus when I ordered her off. And during the horrid experience at the Bien Hoa whorehouse, and the many encounters with the enemy as I shuttled troops back and forth.)

[2]Like America's predecessors in Vietnam, the French, the vietnamese called us "long noses" (or "monky men," because of our substantial body hair, something little known to Vietnamese). Also because the French had worn U.S. style gear, some Vietnamese mistook us for them, believing they had returned.

In addition to their ability to convince peasants and villagers of their nationalistic patriotism, both VC and NVA forces were extremely well trained to fight. This was, after all, an army that had been born into a country that had been battling the French since the late 1800s; not to mention Japanese occupiers during the 1940s. After they'd finally defeated the French in 1954, and the country was partitioned in two by agreement of the Geneva Convention, the government in the south decided it wanted to stay in power. So it threw up roadblocks to a planned election that was supposed to reunify the country in 1956. And by that time, America was backing the South Vietnamese government, just like China and the USSR were backing the one in the north. So, because the south wouldn't go for the election, the Viet Cong, with help from the north, began a revolutionary attempt to unseat the government in the south. With the advent of U.S. military intervention during the mid-1960s, Ho Chi Minh and the Viet Cong saw their struggle to kick out the Americans and unseat the South Vietnamese government as a war of national liberation. We saw it as communist aggression. And, since the "domino theory," first put forward by President Dwight Eisenhower and Vice-President Richard Nixon, dictated that if Vietnam fell to the communists all of Southeast Asia would go the same way, we began pouring in troops.

"The Vietnam War," said President Lyndon B. Johnson, "Will go down in history as the most complex war in all American history."

From the point of view of the grunt on the ground in Nam (and for that matter, any troops confronting the enemy), LBJ was certainly right. Severe difficulty distinguishing Viet Cong guerrillas from ordinary black-clad villagers (most of whom also wanted us out but weren't necessarily pro-communist) caused major havoc for our units. An American soldier couldn't tell a Viet Cong from a Vietnamese nationalist. Guerrillas were often farmers and villagers by day, but by night, fierce and determined enemy fighters. This became the catastrophic problem of the Vietnam War.

And even though they employed a carefully worked out strategy and planned their actions with great deliberation, Ho Chi Minh's forces were willing to fight ten years, twenty years, thirty years or longer if necessary to reach their goal. It didn't seem to matter that much to the Communist Party whether they achieved their success in 1968, 1970, 1975 or the year 2000. Though American officials thought that when Ho Chi Minh died on September 3, 1969, Hanoi's troops might withdraw from the south and that a power struggle would take place in the north, the NVA never skipped a beat. In fact, they seemed more determined to fight on than ever. It didn't seem to matter how many casualties they took, they just kept fighting. As Ho Chi Minh said, among his last words, "Our rivers, our mountains, our men will always remain. The Yanks defeated, we will build our country ten times more beautiful."

North Vietnam's Marxism remained alive, well and flourishing, even after Ho Chi Minh passed on.

In order to identify Vietnamese communist forces from peasants and villagers, the American Central Intelligence Agency (CIA) implemented what they called the "Phoenix Program." This plan, designed to sort out Viet Cong troop leaders and cadre from civilians, didn't exactly work out that way. Many ordinary Vietnamese underwent tremendous suffering because of "Phoenix," and what was regarded as "normal" interrogation in Saigon found ordinary civilians being tortured and occasionally killed. "Phoenix" turned out to be one of the worst kind of antiterrorist programs and one of the most atrocious excesses practiced by the American government.

"Phoenix" corrupted the U.S. military. When reports came in that a suspected Vietnamese was a Viet Cong guerrilla, even though such reports might have no corroboration, at a specific time and on a particular day, a massive B52 air strike would be ordered to wipe out an entire area or Vietnamese village.

This kind of military practice became normal and routine.

With death and destruction all around us, more and more American GIs became traumatized and disillusioned in one way or another, and many soldiers who thought they had been sent to win the hearts and minds of the Vietnamese were losing their own. This was part of the reason, I suppose, why many of us (including me) got caught up in some of the pranks and AWOL escapades we did, like raiding the company kitchens. I also became slightly involved in the black market craze by purchasing a few goods in a military PX and using those to trade for occasional favors in Saigon whorehouses. A "good, clean soldier's mischief" is what I called it. The behavior came out of a mixture of loneliness, grief, frustration and confusion. Often, the resentment we felt and the desire to protest simply resulted in basically honest and decent soldiers taking part in crazy activities such as these.

But some guys did things that were quite atrocious and terribly corrupt; certain GIs made it a regular practice to buy commodities missing on their side of the base's high-wire fence, such as sex, drugs and whatever else wasn't available at the PX. Drugs of all kinds could be had, both on and outside military bases. Many soldiers escaped the hell of military absurdity and frustration by staying high most of the time. Some rear-echelon troops actually lived like warlords, selling or trading goods and equipment on the black market that had been stolen from military bases. Anything that wasn't nailed down could be lifted, even weapons and ammo. Some of these found their way to South Vietnamese district chiefs, or any other corrupt people in authority, who would in turn sell them to VC guerrillas.

Though my own antics were probably minor compared to a lot of GIs, and though they could have caused me serious harm or disciplinary action, at the time, my buddies and I who engaged in these activities didn't think anything that might happen would be serious enough to land us in the LBJ Hotel (the Long Binh Jail). We were young, energetic, restless, lonely, depressed, frustrated with the constant military incompetence we saw all around, and wanting to do all we could to pay back dumb-ass lifers.

For me, maybe wanting to one-up lifers was the main thing. I never minded constructive criticism or the kind of rules we had to obey and the discipline handed down by junior officers and NCOs, but the blatant misuse of military orders and downright incompetence and sheer arrogance on the part of some of these lifers left a lasting impression on me of a false and corrupt system of authority. The kind of harassment too often handed out, was something I despised with a passion.

General George C. Marshall statement from 1944 says it all:

> *The soldier is a man; he expects to be treated as an adult, not a schoolboy. He has rights; they must be made known to him and thereafter respected. He has ambition; it must be stirred. He has a belief in fair play; it must be honored. He has a need of comradeship. It must be supplied. He has imagination; it must be stimulated. He has a sense of personal dignity; it must be sustained. He has pride; it can be satisfied and made the bedrock of character once he has been assured that he is playing a useful and respected role. To give a man this is the acme of inspired leadership. He has become loyal because loyalty was given to him.*

Looking back, now that I'm in my sixties, I'm amazed at some of the crazy things I did then. But that's how it was.

For many of us, the Vietnam War was like walking into an endless maze; you really didn't know where the hell the path was leading, what its real purpose was, and how you'd get out. As a result of this constant emotional confusion, the violence, fragging (assaults on American officers and NCOs by ordinary GIs, often covered up as though it had happened in combat) was believed to be almost fifteen times as great as in the harsh warfare of World War II.

Resentment between races and social classes also swelled, because black and other minority groups and low income or poor young people saw being drafted as additional discrimination, since the U.S. Selective Service system favored those who were able to obtain deferments because they could afford to go to college. In some cases, I'm sure that young men of draft age fell through the cracks because they had wealthy or influential families. Or they happened to rub elbows with very powerful people.[3]

As the war trudged on and on in the later years, so did fragging, soldier on soldier violence, and the questionable and unjustifiable killing of Vietnamese civilians. It was a war of massive atrocities, corruption and putrefaction in every sense of those words.

Nor, it seemed, were the North Vietnamese any better. To most of us, it seemed like there were no "rules

[3]One of the more disgraceful programs designed to pull in recruits for Vietnam was Project 100,000. Under this policy, 100,00 young men who had failed (or would fail if tested) the Army's physical or mental requirements were "given the chance" to become solders. In his book *Military Men*, author Ward Just states that these men, most of them undeducated or illiterate, became part of a "monstrous joke," being forced to struffle through basic training as thy struggled through life generally, and once in combat often became more of a liability than an asset. "A soldier who cannot read or write," he says, "would make a very danerous mortarman."

of battle" during the Vietnam War. Especially when it came to Ho Chi Minh's army. If American troops were captured, they'd better thank the lord they were taken prisoner. Or maybe not, since captivity could often lead to severe and inhuman treatment. Lower ranking troops were often tortured for information. Many captured soldiers never lived to see another day or tell about their capture.[4]

Tactics employed by the Viet Cong were different from anything America had been used to. To gain control over as much of an area as possible, hundreds of small, tightly knit units, called cells, were created. Each cell consisted of from three to a dozen people, all of about the same rank and authority. These well-organized and very dedicated VC cells were able to take almost total control over one small village after another, practically under the noses of our military and of the, ARVN, the South Vietnamese Army. The Viet Cong were masters at disguise and camouflage. It was also extremely hard to pin them down; they used the heat and humidity as an ally, and carefully hiding their well-placed base camps (an old Chinese tactic) was a high guerrilla priority.

To add to the difficulties America had in trying to overcome this vast, strongly disciplined and well organized VC army in the south, some members of our so-called allies in the ARVN would, on occasion, secretly show up at meetings and assist the VC in convincing doubters. Some were certainly sympathetic to the communist cause. Others probably wanted to be sure they were on the winning side, just in case the north prevailed. But with this kind of two-sided game, it was only a matter of time before the Viet Cong's consistent effort gained a powerful stronghold in village after village. It was virtually impossible, I believe, for most of

---

[4] At the war's end, only 591 Americans, mostly pilots were released from captivity.

the civilian peasantry and villagers not to become part of the cause. They didn't really have other options. It wasn't so much that South Vietnamese villagers and the peasants chose the communist movement, as that the movement chose them.

Of course, not every cell was strictly military; some carried out propaganda, others headed up security operations, some administered what was considered justice, and others taught party doctrine. Vietnamese civilians, I believe, joined the communist cause or even the Communist Party for what they saw as a life of freedom and/or glory; for something quite different from the kind of ungratifying lives they'd been experiencing as hardworking peasants or villagers. The communists had a great ability to organize, and to isolate local people from dissenting information. After regular and persistent meetings about Party doctrine, as well as lectures about what would be achieved in terms of land and freedom once the country was rid of Americans, most, I think, became won over.

When education or persuasion became more difficult, assassination of opposition leaders or village chiefs and others was, we heard, used as a fear tactic. Severe punishment after a show trial might include amputation of an arm or leg, and in some cases, a public execution. Perhaps even by beheading, disembowelment or being burned alive. Gory punishments like these would certainly have been very effective in impressing and converting village populations. After such spectacles, any of those still in opposition would quickly fall into line.

While I can't testify that this was official communist policy everywhere, I heard such stories often enough to report with confidence that it did happen. In a war, especially one in which passions became easily inflamed such as in Vietnam, some people on both sides are likely to commit atrocities. We had our own term for what some of these practices on our side turned out to be: "Search and Destroy" missions, or S.A.D., actions designed to whip out enemy concentrations wherever we found them. There seemed to be no question of how "humane" these Search and Destroy missions were. The My Lai massacre was a prime example.[5] Then too, using napalm to burn people alive was widely regarded as an atrocity. Horrible things are done in war, most often in the name of freedom or liberation. (Estimates of the amount of napalm dispersed over Vietnam range as high as 338,000 tons.)

During the mid 1940s to 1950s, while the French still occupied the country, the Vietnamese communists dug an extensive series of underground tunnels all over areas they controlled in South Vietnam. These major underground tunnel systems served a variety of special military purposes: as arsenals, food storage facilities, hospitals, housing, rest and sleeping rooms, training rooms and anything and everything required for fighting a long, hard and strenuous war. While our B-52s and bulldozers destroyed sections of these tunnels, for the most part, they survived. In fact, the Tet Offensive of 1968, the Post-Tet of 1969 and the final attack on Saigon in April 1975 were launched from the VC's labyrinth of tunnels and caves that stretched over an area of about 100,000 acres. The advantages the enemy enjoyed, and which they deployed against our military superpower, were considerable. In the fields, the rice paddies, jungles in and around villages of various sizes, the enemy had many more experienced soldiers than we did. VC and NVA soldiers were not only men, but women and older

---

[5] On March 16, 1968, men of Charlie Company, 11th Brigade, Americal Division, angry and frustrated over many Viet Cong attacks during the preceeding weeks, entered the village of My Lai. "This is what you've been waiting for – search and destroy – and you've got it!" said their officers. Without any evidence that there were VC about, nor any fire directed against them from the village, Charlie Company mercilessly slaughtered over 300 unarmed villagers, including women, children and the elderly.

children as well, and many of these fought for years and years in and around the Vietnamese countryside.

The VC and NVA were also tremendously adept at improvising. In 1966, a Marine grunt learned some alarming information when he personally discovered a large stash of 36,000 U.S. "Bouncing Betty" mines left behind by ARVN troops, and which VC and NVA guerrillas had then found. Apparently, all that had to be done was to pull the pin on the mines and hide or bury them.

The blasters would be buried under light duff and leaves, or placed in shrubbery or trees. In fact, the industrious guerrillas had a ball decorating the jungle with them. If these "Bettys" were stepped on they'd usually go off about waist-high. In fact, the informative Marine said that someone in his squad had actually triggered one, and the poor dude got a load of the shrapnel in the cheeks of his ass. This wounded soldier then went on joking about his million-dollar wound, and that he'd soon be dusted-off in a chopper and it wouldn't be long before he'd be chasing good-looking nurses around in the hospital. He was placed on a stretcher and taken to a medevac chopper, but before reaching the military hospital, while in mid flight, he tragically went into severe shock and died.

Hundreds of such incidents were commonplace during the Vietnam War. We were dealing with an enemy that had improvised since the time the Chinese occupied their land around a thousand years ago. So from the very beginning, we faced a people with many centuries of experience in guerrilla warfare.

Against all this ingenuity, America employed enormous technological superiority (though withholding our trump card, nuclear weapons). In the later years of the war our technology had advanced even more. And so too had the technology, tactics and weaponry of the

North Vietnamese, with the most sophisticated aircraft, and both small and large arms and antiaircraft gunnery being served up by China and the Soviet Union. But back in the spring of 1965, it had seemed as if the war would be a slam-dunk for the vast American war machine. With the overwhelming superiority of our combat troops and advanced technology it seemed that the Vietnamese peasant soldiers equipped with an odd assortment of old, obsolete and primitive small-arms and homemade mines, bombs and booby traps were indeed going to be outgunned, outwitted and ultimately doomed. Our gung-ho politicians and the military brass back in Washington assumed that we'd steamroller these primitive peasants, and that in no time they'd be crushed, worn down to a pitiful frenzy, and be only too happy to sue for peace.

Didn't quite work out that way. By 1973, the North Vietnamese were practically as well equipped and as highly sophisticated in terms of technology as we were.

The greatest asset and most important advantage of the enemy, however, was not Chinese or Soviet arms, not torture, not their unconventional tactics nor their ability to improvise. It was their relentless and unbelievable will to win. Despite the poverty of the Vietnamese, Hanoi's communist army in the 1960's was one of the largest and most tenacious in the world. This was an army willing to suffer massive hardship and sacrifice millions of lives in order to achieve its goals. All that really mattered was to oust or outlast the American military then overrun South Vietnam and finish off its government.

By midsummer of 1969, information had leaked out that the majority of NVA soldiers, both men and women, were of two age groups: those approximate 15 to 18, and those 35 to 50. By that time, most of those in the preferred 19 to 34 age group had been killed off by our massive military onslaught. Since most of those in their best-trained and most experienced age group had been annihilated, the North Vietnamese Communist Party had resorted to using whoever was available. And this seemed to present an increasingly negative reaction among some of the NVA troops. Because of their fear of imminent death, and the high number of casualties they sustained, some began to slowly resist the aggressive fighting.

Of course, the worse things got for us the more that official U.S. reports were prone to enormously inflate the enemy body count, in order to fool American public opinion about the war's progress. So we could never be exactly sure what was going on.

During June and July of 1969, I heard a couple alarming reports from Marine helicopter pilots and door gunners about dead NVA troops having been found chained down into battle positions so as not to be able to flee. In other words these NVA soldiers, perhaps those expected to be deserters, were most likely forced against their will to fight for the communist side or die. This may well have been because their more determined fighters had been wiped out. Then too, many NVA and Viet Cong of all ages were true believers, and may have chosen to chain themselves down simply to prove their dedication. Whichever way it was, the North Vietnamese leadership obviously pulled out all the stops to win.

For the ARVN, the war seemed no big deal. The Vietnamese may not have loved war but it was the hand they'd been dealt. War was not at all new to Vietnam. For twenty centuries, Vietnam had been the graveyard of foreign armies and the Vietnamese alike, so it seemed like for most ARVN troops this was just another thing to go through.

The army of South Vietnam, the ARVN (supposedly our allies), was, for the most part, without much motivation. Their attitude seemed to be, "Why risk dying in a war when the stupid, headstrong American soldier can bear the burden? The American military has the money, the fighting force, the expertise and the will and desire to fight, so why should we lay our lives on the line? The Americans are intruders in our land, so let them do the fighting."

Desertions by South Vietnamese troops, in fact, were twenty-one percent of the total ARVN force! General "Westy" Westmoreland regarded the ARVN soldiers as something of a low capability fighting force. Most actually performed quite well when they had good leadership. But actually, there was a severe shortage of qualified Vietnamese leaders. In my opinion, the South Vietnamese Army lost their ability to fight because most Americans had no patience and would jump in and do things themselves, and this robbed the Vietnamese of self-determination and initiative.

Why do you suppose the United States faired so poorly in its effort to prevail during the war in Vietnam? That's an easy one: the Vietnamese communists had a goal, and in spite of the inhumane behavior by some of them against villagers, or by forcing unseasoned troops to fight, they also had the will of most of the Vietnamese on their side. We had the exact opposite. Few of our soldiers had proper moral support, and the will of the American people was never strongly behind us.

Both at home and among our troops, it was fairly common knowledge that narrow-minded and corrupt individuals, including but not limited to the CIA, military officials and politicians, conspired to direct and rule the war in Vietnam, and that the American people were bamboozled into believing that their honorable military was actually fighting for democracy.

Directed by a military and political conglomerate spreading misinformation and misleading propaganda, America's leadership decided that increasing the number of our troops in Vietnam was more appropriate and necessary than would be the political cost of pulling out in a humiliating disgrace, and possibly inviting new military scrimmages and challenges across the globe.

And the result of this mistaken, hardheaded and thoughtless policy? More and more dead Americans. With the war dragging on and on.

In his insightful work, *About Face*, Colonel David H. Hackworth (U.S. Army, Retired), says we ended up "botching" the war because:

• We didn't require the South Vietnamese government to institute reforms, and allowed corruption to flourish.

• We failed to develop an overall objective and strategic plan.[6]

• We failed to develop small unit tactics that would support an overall campaign plan.

• We never understood the nature of guerrilla warfare.

• We sent a force into Vietnam that was top-heavy with supporters and thin on fighters.

• Senior officers serving in Vietnam had tactical know-how that was deplorable.

• Our central command structure was filled with people who were too abrasive, opinionated, undiplomatic, nonconformist and ineffective.

In short, he felt "second stringers who talk a good

---

[6] One survey revealed that of the Army generals who had "managed" the war in Vietnam, almost 70 percent were uncertain of its objectives.

game in the shower room and are adroit at fixing the blame on others" ran much of the operation The entire system, he goes on, "desperately needs an enema." One that will have to be initiated from outside the army.

I couldn't agree more.

Eventually, of course – and in spite of what the American military *didn't* do – it came down to the determined will and passions of the North Vietnamese people and their Viet Cong allies, the people the communists called "the engines of war." This idea about the Vietnamese people being the "engines of war" seemed to give the enemy all they needed to win. Without this determination, they certainly would have failed.

Our "engines of war," our brave but often demoralized troops, had no such goals, only a never clearly defined idea that we were "fighting for democracy." So it was hardly surprising that over the course of this long, hard war, we ran out of steam. Disgusted, disgruntled and frustrated American serviceman never had a clear line on the enemy, nor a solid objective that seemed worthy of the ultimate sacrifice.

Additionally, our government had continued to support the war under the delusion that a victorious outcome was quite possible without the popular support of the American people. So the serviceman in Vietnam fought on and on, with more and more troops pouring into the country, and more and more dying. While all the time, our government underestimated our very determined and ferociously fighting enemy, "the little people." And we overestimated our own military expertise.

By the time the war was over and the fat lady sang, more than 3.2 million American men and women served in Southeast Asia from the time of America's first significant involvement in Vietnam in 1961, until the last Americans left in April of 1975.

The Vietnam War was the longest, most controversial, most costly, most misguided and most misunderstood conflict in American military history. The Viet Cong and North Vietnamese Army tested the endurance, patience and the understanding of America's citizens in ways that other wars have not. More than 58,000 men and women sacrificed their lives, and more than 150,000 were seriously wounded in Vietnam, in what is now widely regarded as having been a meaningless, wasteful and unnecessary crusade. When the smoke of war cleared and sober analysis became possible, we learned that over $150 billion U.S. dollars had been squandered. In addition to the enormous expenditure of money and personnel that was exhausted by the outrageously imbecilic and overzealous operations carried out by the Central Intelligence Agency's covert actions in Vietnam's bordering countries, Laos and Cambodia.

The war in Vietnam – an American tragedy. And quite possibly a bright, shinning lie from the beginning. Every point of view should be studied, examined, mulled over, taught and explored by future generations. And through looking at and understanding our tragic past, the American people should develop and discover new and non-aggressive strategies to resolve differences, and hopefully attain peace all around the world without bloodshed and death.

The suffering that came out of Vietnam, for both veterans and their families, goes well beyond the official numbers of those killed and wounded.

Unlike veterans of other wars, America's Vietnam serviceman came home alone. There were no patriotic parades, no flags waving as vets, their chests swelling with pride, marched down Main Street. Instead of celebrations acknowledging their sacrifice, many serviceman were confronted at airports and on streets and parks throughout the United States with a despicable welcoming party, a bombardment of unsympathetic protests by hippies, longhairs and flower children carrying vulgar signs. Some even went to the extent of cursing and throwing objects at the troops, as had happened to me when I landed in California. Not that all protesters behaved like this, but a strong and vocal minority certainly did. And this was sad, because right or wrong, we had given up our time, our freedom, our families, our health, and for tens of thousands, our very lives. I must ask how much damn blood did the soldiers who fought in Vietnam have to spill before they could receive any kind of appreciation or recognition for their sacrifice? What kind of thanks and what kind of hospitality did we get for our effort? The answer is clear.

This treatment even extended to the "war dogs" employed in Vietnam. Over the course of the war, some 4000 dogs and 10,000 handlers worked in Nam. Dogs were used as sentries, scouts, to detect ambushes or snipers, as messengers and to find mines and tunnels. They saved thousands of American lives. Sadly, and deliberately, these loyal war dogs were left behind and given to the South Vietnamese Army. Many troops who had trained and worked with these dogs wanted to take them home to the U.S., but the brass wouldn't allow it. The dogs and handlers deserved much better.

And I have to say that I don't feel good about what "Hanoi Jane" Fonda did during the war. It's fine that she wanted to oppose America's involvement. Millions did. She even went around entertaining GIs on leave with her FTA show. But for her to have visited North Vietnam and pose on an antiaircraft battery, and to utter some of the statements she made, I found truly deplorable. I honesty can't find it in my heart to forgive her for such disrespectful behavior. While I'm aware that Fonda has apologized for the form her protests against the war took, I'm not in the least surprised that so many Vietnam vets, particularly former POWs, continue to retain such bitter feelings toward her.

Among too many Americans, Vietnam veterans have had an unfair image as baby butchers, warmongers, or at the very least, social outcasts and misfits. Many years after the war was over, many vets were seen as emotionally unstable, having severe nervous disorders and being incapable of adjusting to the real world outside of the jungles, fields and villages of war-torn Vietnam.

And, in fact, for a large number, this has been true.

It's been estimated that 500,000 to 700,000 Vietnam-era veterans have suffered from "post-traumatic stress disorder" (P.T.S.D.) The symptoms range from depression, nervousness, remembering horrible combat experiences, to a sense of guilt at having made it home alive and survived the war, when thousands and thousands of other men did not. This was, in fact – although it wasn't called that at the time – the disorder I was diagnosed with by the Oakland army doctors on my return.

In Vietnam, venereal disease afflicted more soldiers than in any previous American conflict. Towards the end of the war, V.D. was the most common diagnosable ailment. Approximately 260 out of every 1,000 men contracted one variety or another of this debilitating condition.

Additionally, many soldiers in Vietnam had been exposed to Agent Orange, a defoliant spray used extensively throughout the war during the 1960s and into the early 70's. There has been overwhelming evidence to suggest that exposure to this defoliant causes skin rashes, and possible birth defects in children, and the probability that it causes various cancers.

To be more specific, over the past decade the numbers of diseases the Veterans Administration has recognized as associated with, but not necessarily caused by exposure to Agent Orange and other herbicides, has expanded considerably. The conditions now recognized as service connected for war veterans with service in Vietnam from 1962 to 1975 include: chloracne, a skin condition that resembles acne; acute and subacute porphyria cutanea tarda – a disorder involving liver and skin problems; peripheral neuropathy – a nervous system condition that causes numbness and tingling; type II diabetes; and numerous cancers, including Hodgkin's disease, non-Hodgkin's lymphoma, certain soft tissue sarcomas, multiple myeloma, prostate cancer, respiratory cancer, lung cancer, bronchus, larynx or trachea, and chronic lymphatic leukemia.

Furthermore, children born of Vietnam War veterans exposed to Agent Orange have been diagnosed with the birth defect spina bifida. Additionally, a wide range of other birth defects have been discovered in children who were born to female Vietnam War veterans.[7]

To personalize the above, for many years since Vietnam I've suffered from a variety of health concerns, including nervous system disorders (including slight numbness and tingling), prostrate troubles, and a constantly recurring skin rash. For all of these, I continue to take a variety of prescribed medications. And to top it off, I've discovered over the years that I'm extremely susceptible to colds and flu.

Agent Orange? Well, while I'm still in the process of trying to make the connection, I do all I can to combat the possible effects. Mainly by isolating myself at my Montana ranch.

---

[7] It's important to note that under VA policy, every Vietnam War veteran is "assumed" to have been exposed to Agent Orange.

In my strong view, the Veterans Administration has basically turned it's back on the Vietnam veteran and failed to come up to the plate in dealing with both Agent Orange and P.T.S.D.–related problems. Personally, I believe the V.A. plans to stall as long as possible and procrastinate until so much time has passed that enough veterans who have filed disability claims related to P.T.S.D or Agent Orange will either die off or eventually give up on their claims out of disgust and sheer frustration. Angered by years of delay, the American Legion and Vietnam Veterans of America have been waging a long and often frustrating battle to combat foot dragging over studies to ascertain the effects of Agent Orange. Foot dragging that many believe has been orchestrated by the White House. (Because of fear of the immense cost to the government if it's proved that Agent Orange is the cause of many unexplained illnesses among veterans.)

My gut feeling tells me we'd probably have been much further ahead and better off as a nation if America had left the poor, downtrodden Vietnamese people alone and kept our noses completely out of their country in the first place.

I need to ask a couple of very big questions here: what were we fighting for in Vietnam, and who was our real enemy? If we, the soldiers, the veterans of the Vietnam War, and the American people fully understood and really knew the depth of the answer to that question, and the real truth, then we might understand why the United States lost the longest and grimmest war we've ever fought.

Regrettably, America, and particularly our government and military, don't seem to have drawn too many lessons from the multitude of mistakes that were made and that led to the most significant military defeat in our long history. As citizens, we can no longer afford to be the armed policeman of the entire free world, fight everyone we hate or even disagree with, or resolve every dispute that comes along through force of arms. On the other hand, I'm in full agreement that we need strong national security. When the time is right to wage war, we need to wage it. And wage it with a passion that is just and final.

And what about me? Am I sorry about the things I did in Nam and the way in which I served the United States Army and my country? I really can't answer that with absolute certainty. Sometimes I think that I was caught up between being a "patriot" and "protester." Mostly, I favor being patriotic. I definitely believe in national security, but after thinking back on all that went on in Vietnam, I begin to more fully understand all the protests.

Beyond all the bullshit that went on during the war, and even considering some of the outrageous things I did, I think I was a pretty conscientious and fairly good soldier. I believe I represent what average American GIs were like, generally doing my work in a responsible and trustworthy way. Especially performing duties such as driving a bus and transporting thousands of troops. I did what I was ordered to do by my superiors and did it well.

I was honorably discharged as a Specialist 4th Class. No frills, no Silver Star or Bronze Star, just the regular stuff like the Good Conduct Medal, National Defense Service Medal and the Vietnam Campaign Medal.

But I'm also glad that I had only two years of active duty. Incompetence and corruption were a serious problem within the entire military in Vietnam. Poor leadership and lousy judgment were common among junior officers, and on occasion among NCOs and higher brass. Which is not to say that all or most NCOs and officers were incompetent. In fact, there were a much higher percentage of decent and well-qualified ones among these ranks than there were of the opposite. It's simply that in a barrel of apples, the rotten ones always seem to stand out – and often contaminate the rest.

How many names on the big black granite wall at the Vietnam War Memorial are actually there because those troops went into battle knowing full well what they were getting into and what they were up against? And how many are there because they were victims of a flawed, corrupt, and manipulated intelligence system? Many a brave American serviceman, ordered by a commanding officer, was cut down with precision, almost as if he was the victim of a street gang firing squad, and sentenced to death by their executioner.

We, the American soldiers, fought the war for many long, grudging years, but in my opinion, the United States, even being the super power it was in terms of sophisticated fire power, strategy, intelligence and expertise, let us all down both militarily and in general, and the war was fought helter-skelter. Because every instance of American military failure brought forth the blatant excuse that more troops would do the job, more bombs and guns and airplanes would hasten inevitable victory.

The war in Vietnam was truly a lame duck and a military blunder!

The hubris generated by the American government that came with our great victory in World War II was most likely a major contributing factor to the thrust into Vietnam. Nonetheless, we the American people can now take from World War II a big and important lesson and apply it to Vietnam: we need not become cocky and overconfident as we did in Vietnam. And as we did again in Iraq during the second Gulf War. And we should never forget the soldiers that didn't make it back. We need to honor and respect all those who served. But especially those who did not return, and those who returned physically or mentally disabled.

Americans are still paying a massive price in many ways for our involvement in Vietnam and it's unfortunate miscalculations. The Wall, the Vietnam War Memorial in Washington, D.C., lists the names of every merican killed in Vietnam. It's a beautiful monument, an honorable tribute to brotherhood and a moving testament to those heroic and patriotic serviceman who paid the ultimate price for America's involvement in that tragic and unnecessary war. Let's hope we learn from our mistakes. Let's hope we learn not to repeat them.

And let us also hope that each of us can learn not to repeat our own mistakes. After Vietnam, I had to go through a hell of a lot, personally, to discover a better way to live. It took me more years than I like to think about. Decades of trial and error in business, in relationships, in continuing hassles with government. It doesn't seem like I'd gain a lot by beating my chest or dwelling on some of the stupid or thoughtless things I did. They just were. And I certainly take responsibility for them. Many of my problems came out of the war, others were probably stuff that was never resolved during my early life, and some was entirely of my own making. As I look back on all the miserable trouble I've been through myself, and some I've piled on others, I know it's important to keep trying to do better. I'm not sure I've learned enough yet about how to do that, because I still don't always succeed in everything I try. But I do know that I'm on the way.

I look back to the question posed by the title of this book: *Who's My Enemy*? Have I answered that? Perhaps not, I'm not sure. In a way, I suppose that each of us, soldier and non-soldier alike, have to make our own peace with that question, draw our own conclusions, and figure out how much of what happened to us has been brought on by circumstance, and how much we've brought on ourselves. I still look at that frequently, trying to figure it all out.

One thing I do know, however: the Wall helped to heal me. I hope it can help to heal America. No thorn, no trial or tribulation however painful can diminish our zeal for life and freedom. May our zeal likewise continue strong.

As the troops used to say . . . Keep the Faith!

YEAR 1995. LYNN BOWMAN AT MONTANA RANCH.
JUDITH RIVER IN BACKGROUND

WHO'S MY ENEMY?

WHO'S MY ENEMY?

More from Nordskog Publishing...

PREPARE A ROOM:
A Path to Peace and Healing for Those Hurt by Abortion
by Michelle Shelfer

A CULTURE OF DENIAL about the traumatic effects of abortion has left many women and men trapped in regret, shame, and self-condemnation about their experience. How can those who have been traumatized by this deeply wounding scourge find a doorway to freedom and hope? Michelle Shelfer offers a ten-step path to peace and healing that addresses the damage done to identity and relationships and offers real-life tools to restore what has been broken. Embark on a journey that honors your unique story and opens the door to restoration through discovery of the greatest love.